Mentoring is a Verb

This accessible guide offers school leaders a wealth of strategies to foster a culture where educators engage with young people to encourage college readiness and career success. Based on research and best practices, *Mentoring is a Verb* explains how to build effective mentoring programs as well as encourage educators to individually mentor students. Olwell breaks down the key elements it takes to forge lasting relationships with students and addresses ways to connect with at-risk students. Packed with actionable steps, this book gives you the tools to help your students set high expectations and goals, recognize and address barriers to success, plan for the future, and reach their post-graduation aspirations.

Russ Olwell is Director of the Institute for the Study of Children, Families, and Communities and Professor of History at Eastern Michigan University, USA. He has worked in summer programs, as a middle school teacher, and as Director of EMU GEAR UP, a pre-college program that sent more than 600 high school students in low-income districts to college.

Other Eye On Education Books Available from Routledge
(www.routledge.com/eyeoneducation)

How to Make Data Work: A Guide for Educational Leaders
Jenny Grant Rankin

A School Leader's Guide to Implementing the Common Core: Inclusive Practices for All Students
Gloria Campbell-Whatley, Dawson Hancock, and David M. Dunaway

What Connected Educators Do Differently
Todd Whitaker, Jeffrey Zoul, and Jimmy Casas

BRAVO Principal! Building Relationships with Actions that Value Others, 2nd Edition
Sandra Harris

Get Organized! Time Management for School Leaders, 2nd Edition
Frank Buck

The Educator's Guide to Writing a Book: Practical Advice for Teachers and Leaders
Cathie E. West

Data, Data Everywhere: Bringing All the Data Together for Continuous School Improvement, 2nd Edition
Victoria Bernhardt

Leading Learning for Digital Natives: Combining Data and Technology in the Classroom
Rebecca J. Blink

The Trust Factor: Strategies for School Leaders
Julie Peterson Combs, Stacey Edmonson, and Sandra Harris

The Assistant Principal's Guide: New Strategies for New Responsibilities
M. Scott Norton

The Principal as Human Resources Leader: A Guide to Exemplary Practices for Personnel Administration
M. Scott Norton

Formative Assessment Leadership: Identify, Plan, Apply, Assess, Refine
Karen L. Sanzo, Steve Myran, and John Caggiano

Easy and Effective Professional Development: The Power of Peer Observation to Improve Teaching
Catherine Beck, Paul D'Elia, and Michael W. Lamond

Job-Embedded Professional Development: Support, Collaboration, and Learning in Schools
Sally J. Zepeda

Leading Schools in an Era of Declining Resources
J. Howard Johnston and Ronald Williamson

Creating Safe Schools: A Guide for School Leaders, Teachers, and Parents
Franklin P. Schargel

Mentoring is a Verb

Strategies for Improving College and Career Readiness

Russ Olwell

Routledge
Taylor & Francis Group
NEW YORK AND LONDON

First published 2016
by Routledge
711 Third Avenue, New York, NY 10017

and by Routledge
2 Park Square, Milton Park, Abingdon, Oxon, OX14 4RN

Routledge is an imprint of the Taylor & Francis Group, an informa business

© 2016 Taylor & Francis

The right of Russ Olwell to be identified as author of this work has
been asserted by him in accordance with sections 77 and 78 of the
Copyright, Designs and Patents Act 1988.

Trademark notice: Product or corporate names may be trademarks or
registered trademarks, and are used only for identification and
explanation without intent to infringe.

Library of Congress Cataloging in Publication Data
Names: Olwell, Russ, author.
Title: Mentoring is a verb : strategies for improving college and
career readiness / Russ Olwell.
Description: New York, NY : Routledge, [2016] | Includes
bibliographical references.
Identifiers: LCCN 2015030496| ISBN 9781138930162 (hardback) |
ISBN 9781138930179 (pbk.) | ISBN 9781315680699 (ebook)
Subjects: LCSH: Mentoring in education. | College preparation
programs. | School-to-work transition.
Classification: LCC LB1731.4 .O495 2016 | DDC 371.102--dc23LC
record available at http://lccn.loc.gov/2015030496

ISBN: 978-1-138-93016-2 (hbk)
ISBN: 978-1-138-93017-9 (pbk)
ISBN: 978–1-315-68069-9 (ebk)

Typeset in Optima
by Florence Production Ltd, Stoodleigh, Devon, UK

Printed and bound in the United States of America by Publishers Graphics,
LLC on sustainably sourced paper.

*To my wife, Mary, and my
daughter, Laurea Lucy*

Contents

Meet the Author

Russ Olwell is Director of the Institute for the Study of Children, Families, and Communities and Professor of History at Eastern Michigan University, USA. He has worked in summer programs, as a middle school teacher, as a professor of history education, and has served on a school board.

From 2006–2012, Olwell directed EMU GEAR UP, a pre-college program that sent more than 600 high school students in three low-income districts to college, working with these students from seventh to twelfth grades to build academic skills, as well as knowledge of the admissions and financial aid processes. He has written scholarly articles for the *History Teacher*, as well as such popular outlets as *KDP Record, OAH Magazine of History*, and *AHA Perspectives*. He has published commentaries in *Education Week*, the *Chronicle of Higher Education* and *Inside Higher Ed* (online).

Preface

You want to make a difference.

In your school building, or community center, or faith community, you see that young people are not reaching the potential that they could. Some of the young people in the community are not doing as well as their parents did, and even graduating from high school does not seem to be the sure thing that it was a generation ago.

You, like other people in your community, are willing to invest more time with young people to help them get unstuck and to move ahead. But it is hard to decide when to intervene. Should you be helping students in middle school to make better choices, or should you aim for the high school students who seem most at risk? Would a program aimed at one group, like young men, have the greatest impact?

This book is about how to make a difference in the life of a young person, either as an individual mentor or as part of a program. This book aims to bring you some of the research in the field to help you think about what you might want to do, as well as some practices that leading mentoring programs use to shape their work. Mentoring is much like cooking, and so you will need to vary the recipe based on your location and the young people with whom you are working.

Research on mentoring shows us that there is a real potential to do good in mentoring programs but also a potential to harm young people, particularly when the adults in the program lack responsibility and reliability. Throughout the book, the focus will be on enhancing the good we can do and avoiding the harm that can come from poor or uneven mentoring relationships.

Mentoring young people is hard work, and it has its ups and downs over the years. Young people into whom you have invested a great deal of time and effort can disappoint you, and you have to be patient watching over them as they mature. Long-term mentoring programs and relationships can seem like the story of the prodigal son. A participant can disappear for a while, giving the mentor a scare, and then reappear.

Intended Audience

I wrote this book to help people mentor, ether as individuals or as part of a program. It is intended to help novices to the field, as well as those who are well into the process to improve their craft. While there are cautions given in the book, particularly about the negative impacts of poor mentoring programs, this work is intended to encourage people to take on mentoring opportunities, and to look for ways to make a difference in the lives of young people.

This book is intended for anyone who mentors now, anyone who is thinking of starting as a mentor or starting a program, and anyone who wants to improve a mentoring effort. There are some critical groups I have aimed to address as the audience of this book:

1. School leaders, whether staff or teachers, who have a tremendous opportunity to make a difference in the lives of young people through mentoring.
2. People who work in support roles at school, in student-success programs, or in after-school programs. These individuals often interact with students in a one-on-one way that teachers no longer have the time to. As a result, they can help shape the trajectory that young people take.
3. Students interested in mentoring as part of becoming a professional in education, social work, or other human services fields.

But good mentors come from all walks of life, and from all different backgrounds—I am hoping that anyone interested in mentoring will find what follows to be of interest.

Structure of the Book

This book is divided into five parts. After an introduction (Chapter 1), Part 1 (Chapters 2–7) examines what mentoring is, both in terms of traditional definitions and recent research in the field. Part 2 (Chapters 8–10) examines the forces that mentors are up against, and Part 3 (Chapters 11–15) gives strategies for people and programs to overcome these barriers. Part 4 (Chapters 16 and 17) discusses mentoring and mentoring programs over the long haul, and Part 5 (Chapters 18–20) looks at ways to sustain mentoring programs over time. While many themes of the book run through multiple chapters, the chapters were written to allow readers or programs to skip around and focus on the key elements that they need to address now, saving other pieces for later.

Description of the Chapters

Chapter 1: Mentoring Young People towards Post-Secondary Success

This chapter sets the context for mentoring programs, asking whether the high school diploma is enough for today's students. The chapter then looks at what programs can help encourage young people to find success after high school and the ways adults can support the dreams of young people through mentoring. The chapter also looks at research on what really helps young people attend and succeed in college or other high-quality post-secondary options.

Chapter 2: What Does It Mean to Be a Mentor for Young People?

Homer's *Odyssey* is the book that gave us the concept of "mentor." This chapter draws from the *Odyssey* and other sources to look at the multiple roles that mentors play in the lives of young people.

Chapter 3: What Mentoring Can and Cannot Do

There is a solid base of research on the positive and negative impacts that mentoring programs can have. This chapter will explain what researchers have learned about mentoring, and how to apply this to designing a good mentoring program or establishing a solid mentoring relationship.

Chapter 4: Setting Up Programs and Relationships the Right Way

This chapter addresses the ways that good mentoring bonds and programs are designed. It includes information on who should and should not serve as a mentor, as well as ways to help build solid pairs or groups of mentors/ mentees. It will also include nuts and bolts information on keeping mentoring programs and relationships safe.

Chapter 5: Barriers and Limits to Mentoring

Young people face a variety of risk factors, including violence, inadequate education, poor family support, and health issues. This chapter will briefly overview these and will discuss the risks that young people take in their teenage years, using survey research.

Chapter 6: Starting at "Ground Zero": The Issues Young Men Face

Young men, particularly young men of color, face almost overwhelming odds in their quest to graduate from high school, advance their education afterward, and start a rewarding career. This chapter will address the issue of why young men face such challenges as crime, poor schools, and pressure to engage in violence, and the risks that teen parenthood can have for young men.

Chapter 7: "You Gotta Push": Mentoring Young Women to Success

Young women, while academically achieving at higher rates than young men, also face substantial risk factors in their teen years. This chapter will balance a discussion of the achievement, strength, and support young women currently have with a portrait of the risks that they face in terms of crime, violence, health, and potential pregnancy.

Chapter 8: Setting and Keeping High Expectations

Young people profit greatly from high expectations, but it is not always clear how to relay those expectations. This chapter will include information on setting goals with mentees and helping mentees develop plans based on these expectations. It will also include information on how to avoid slippage in expectations, when mentors and mentees accept sub-par performance.

Chapter 9: Asking Questions to Clarify Goals

This chapter describes various techniques to help young people discuss their dreams, hopes, and fears more openly. It will include some "opening moves" and activities to break the ice, some questions to steer the conversation more deeply, and some last-ditch questions to ask when things are not going as planned. These questions will be drawn from master mentors in the community.

Chapter 10: Connecting to Parents and Guardians

Young people do not always have the family support that mentors would hope for. This chapter will help mentors understand the resources and struggles that parents and guardians face today, and the difficulties they encounter trying to help their young people navigate a system more complex than the one in which they were raised.

Chapter 11: Mapping Out a Plan with a Mentee

Young people often struggle to put their plans into words. This chapter will address how to help young people develop goals and then map those out to become a plan. The chapter will show some examples of student plans and discuss how to help students get their own ideas onto paper.

Chapter 12: Exposure to College Options and Choices

A key activity of mentoring is to bring young people to places they have never been before. When young people talk about programs, field trips are almost always listed as the most valuable experiences. This chapter talks about bringing young people to new places and how to use the trip to get them to reflect on what they might want to do in the future.

Chapter 13: Nuts and Bolts of College Application

Applying for college is a mystery for many families. This chapter will cook down the elements of applying into a few easy steps, keyed to holidays for deadlines. It will also help mentors understand the research on college admissions and guide their mentees to appropriate institutions. The chapter provides advice on how to help young people think about their own decisions and how to help them follow through on commitments they have made, into the enrollment process and even into the first year of college.

Chapter 14: College Aspirations and Affordability: Young People and Financial Aid

College affordability is among the most difficult subjects to raise with students and parents. This chapter will provide a step-by-step process to talk to mentees and their families about choosing a college that is affordable and ethical in its treatment of students. The chapter will also provide resources for mentors and mentees to use to evaluate affordability and facilitate the search for scholarships.

Chapter 15: When College Is Not the Right Choice Right Now

While mentors should hold high expectations for every student, there are many students for whom a two- or four-year academic degree is not the right choice at the time. This chapter details strategies for talking about post-secondary options that are not college, and how to help students navigate their choices. In many cases, career-oriented programs—offered as apprenticeships, internships, or certificate programs at community colleges—are a better fit for some students, particularly those who have family responsibilities.

Chapter 16: Hang in There! Mentoring Through Crises in Young People's Lives

Mentoring relationships have good times and bad. This chapter includes advice on how to stick with a relationship when it is challenging and how to know when to end a mentoring relationship. This chapter will also discuss the different motivations for mentoring, and how programs can help increase and sustain motivation across time.

Chapter 17: When Mentoring Relationships Change

This chapter will discuss milestones in a mentoring relationship and ways to celebrate small and big successes. It will also describe how to celebrate community investment in young people with low-cost, low-stress events.

This includes understanding the difference between "mentor" and "colleague," and how to know when to transition relationships from one to the other. It will describe some ways to mark "graduation" from mentoring to being a colleague and the positive outcomes of successfully making this transition.

Chapter 18: How to Know You Are Making a Difference

This chapter will introduce evaluation tools for mentoring programs, focusing on those that are simple and cost-effective. It also spotlights evaluation approaches that can give you immediate feedback on how to change your program to be more successful.

Chapter 19: Get the Word Out! Marketing Mentoring Programs

It is no longer enough for programs to be successful: program organizers also need to let people know the good work that they are doing. This chapter will introduce some tools for marketing mentoring programs, with a focus on keeping others in the know about activities and outcomes.

Chapter 20: Finding Resources for Mentoring Programs

Every program has needs that it cannot meet at the moment. This chapter covers some basic strategies for obtaining needed resources, including grants, gifts, fundraisers, and other options.

Book Features

Each chapter includes some special features to help apply the concepts in the book to real situations, and to start discussions among groups using the book together.

1. **Real People**: indicated by a small graphic of people, these will be short features on a mentor.
2. **Tie to Leadership**: indicated by a graphic of a knot, these will be short sections highlighting a connection to school leadership practice, an issue under debate in the field, or a research finding in the field relevant to the topic under discussion.

3. **Conversation Starters**: indicated by a word balloon, these will be short questions and topics that can be used to start discussions with young people.
4. **Reflection**: indicated by a mirror graphic, these questions will help mentors reflect on their own experiences in and out of education.
5. **Resources**: each chapter will contain a comprehensive list of books, articles, online, and other useful resources associated with the topic.

A Promise to the Reader

By the end of this book . . .

Reading and applying this book will give you tools to effectively reach out to young people and help them attain their own dream of college or other post-secondary educational options, either individually or through a program. The book will give you a clearer idea of the issues that young people face and strategies to help young people surmount barriers. The book will give you and your program staff the latest research on mentoring, as well as practical tips to apply to future mentoring practice. Finally, the book will give you some ideas about how to create a program that is sustainable over time and has the resources to do its work well.

Acknowledgments

A wide variety of people helped out on this project. Some of these are my colleagues, such as Ron Williamson, Alejandro Baldwin, Pierre Rice, Melissa Calabrese, Kelli Hatfield, Caleb Boswell, Kathy Couture, Jaclyn Stevens, and many others who worked with young people as part of the EMU GEAR UP program. Lynn Malinoff, Scott Teasdale and others at the EMU Bright Futures program have taught me a lot about running powerful youth programs. The staff of EMU Upward Bound (Jennifer Fong, Stephanie Hawkes, Kim Rankins, and Haley Mulka) provided help on college applications and financial aid. Alethea Helbig provided epic proofreading services, and Abigail Kemp and Katrina Humen corrected many errors.

Introduction

Mentoring Young People towards Post-Secondary Success

You know, sometimes I'll go to an eighth-grade graduation and there's all that pomp and circumstance and gowns and flowers. And I think to myself, "It's just eighth grade." To really compete, they need to graduate high school, and then they need to graduate college, and they probably need a graduate degree too. An eighth-grade education doesn't cut it today. Let's give them a handshake and tell them to get their butts back in the library!

Barack Obama, June 15, 2008

Mentoring To and Mentoring Away From

Mentoring needs a direction. Without goals to strive for, mentoring programs are support groups, helping people endure and cope, not overcome. Some programs aim to mentor young people towards a positive path (such as college or a career); others aim to mentor young people away from more negative directions (such as juvenile crime). Both of these approaches are valid and their efforts can overlap. But this book focuses on mentoring that works to help young people attain their own goal of post-secondary education and careers.

Programs that have a singular focus, such as college, have a better chance of success because activities can be better planned, and results can be more accurately measured. To give examples, programs such as Upward Bound and GEAR UP (Gaining Early Awareness and Readiness for Undergraduate Programs) have an explicit goal in mind: successful application to, enrollment in, and completion of college. These programs certainly work best when participants share the program's goals, and they are not designed to work with every single young person. But the program's goals help structure its activities, and the results are more easily measured.

Why Getting Beyond High School Is Vital

Getting our children to graduate from high school is no longer enough in American education for the vast majority of families. Almost everyone will need some education or training beyond high school at some point in their career, and young people need to get in the habit of constantly improving their professional skills. For my grandparents, graduating from eighth grade was a significant achievement. My grandfather dropped out of high school to support his family in the Great Depression, meeting the expectations at the time for young men. Now, he and my grandmother would not be considered middle school graduates but high school dropouts, and federal programs would seek to enroll them in GED or other high school-completion programs.

My own parents' academic achievements just a generation ago—a father with a BA in social work and a mother with a degree from a community college—while good for their neighborhood in Queens, would no longer be considered enough by many who point to the need for students to finish a bachelor's degree and attend graduate or professional school. With many people in the workplace scrambling to add credentials and skills to their resumes (and LinkedIn pages), my parents' career path—work at one work-place for decades—would seem stultifying or economically infeasible.

Over the past decade, the goal of moving students through the K–12 (kinder-garten to twelfth grade) system, graduating them with a diploma, and then expecting them to be able to find a job that provides for economic self-sufficiency, has dimmed. Young people themselves recognize the importance of graduating from high school with a diploma (not a GED), and moving on to college or some form of vocational training. While young people would like to contribute economically to their family through work, they recognize that the jobs that they can get without college are not a long-term solution to their family's economic problems. Even while they may look for work and delay schooling to help their family, they continue to hold college as a long-term dream, if a dream deferred.

GEAR UP programs are designed to get students both excited about and ready for college. In our GEAR UP program, located in three low-income school districts in southeastern Michigan, we originally thought we would need to build motivation for attending college among students and their parents. But in our first surveys, we learned that more than 80 percent of students in seventh grade already held college as a goal, and more than

80 percent of their parents did as well. While students and parents were on the same page about college as a goal, their teachers did not view them as college material, estimating that only half as many of them (40 percent) would get to college.

The changing economy reinforces the need to build skills beyond high school. Jobs that require a bachelor's degree are on the increase, as are "mid-skill" jobs that require some form of post-high school training or apprenticeship. In contrast, jobs that require limited skills or that are filled by people without even high school credentials are decreasing rapidly in numbers (Carnevale & Rose, 2015).

 **REFLECTION**

— What attitudes did you encounter about college in your family and neighborhood?
— What is similar and different between those attitudes and those the young people you work with may have heard?

Encouraging the Next Steps

Efforts to get more young people to attend college date back over 50 years, to Sputnik and the War on Poverty. Upward Bound was founded in 1954 to help highly motivated high school students in low-income high schools graduate and attend college. Our Upward Bound program at Eastern Michigan University (EMU) in Ypsilanti, Michigan, serves 89 students in grades 9–12, as well as their families. More recent federal programs such as GEAR UP have worked to help entire grades of middle school students (usually a seventh grade) undertake a six-year march to college, often taking on hundreds or thousands of students in one program. (Our program at EMU had 1,200 seventh graders at the start.) Recent efforts such as the National College Access Network have sought to move whole twelfth-grade classes into college.

States have also undertaken ambitious changes to high school graduation requirements to try to boost college going. Based on the research of Clifford Adelman, states have required more mathematics classes to graduate from high school, more difficult coursework, and even taking math in twelfth grade to create a "toolbox" that offers the best odds of attending and succeeding in college. Adelman's research (Adelman, 2006) showed that "of all pre-college curricula, the highest level of mathematics one studies in secondary school has the strongest continuing influence on bachelor's degree completion. Finishing a course beyond the level of Algebra 2 (for example, trigonometry or pre-calculus) more than doubles the odds that a student who enters post-secondary education will complete a bachelor's degree."

 ## TIE TO LEADERSHIP

Clifford Adelman's study, *The toolbox revisited* (2006), had the following findings about high school curricula:

- The high school curricula that students take better predicts their graduation from college than their test scores or GPA (grade point average).
- The importance of curriculum is higher for African-American and Latino students than for white students.
- Students from a low SES (socio-economic status) background who attend a school with a strong curriculum perform better in college than the average high SES student.

No Easy Answers

All of the above efforts have run up against significant barriers that are often glossed over by politicians and educational policy makers. The schools that low-income students attend do not produce students who are "prepared" for many of the colleges to which they aspire. While students in low-income schools hope to attend selective colleges, and their GPAs can be at the level expected, standardized test scores lag, often far below what selective state institutions expect. While individual teachers and staff may struggle heroically to help students make this jump to college, the poorly functioning school system means that students ready to pursue their own aspirations are the exception at these schools.

While schools are part of the problem, families and neighborhoods can serve as barriers to students' college going as well. The chaotic nature and complexity of American family life has meant that many parents and caregivers struggle with their own lives, never mind being able to positively impact the lives of their children. Despite high expectations and good intentions, many parents, grandparents, aunts, uncles, and other caregivers struggle to effectively help their children make a jump educationally that they themselves may not have made successfully.

The decline of blue-collar employment in many areas has pulled many neighborhoods into desperate circumstances. The new "lean enterprises" of today have shed many of the blue-, pink-, and white-collar jobs that meant the difference between poverty and prosperity for communities. This means that the financial and social resources that previous generations of students could rely upon are no longer there to support college and its tuition.

CONVERSATION STARTERS

— How do you think your education and career will be different from those of your parents?

— What trends do you see that may make your path different from theirs?

Students and their choices form another considerable barrier to college. While students profess high ambitions for themselves in terms of college and professional school, their day-to-day behavior sometimes does not match these goals. Choices based on the pursuit of popularity and celebrity, poor judgment that leads to unsafe behavior, and the use of violence to solve conflicts can all derail students' academic careers.

These barriers—school, family, students, neighborhoods—are formidable. No program that works with young people can underestimate their impact. Policies that ignore these factors are doomed, or at least bound to be taught some hard lessons. Those who implement programs without respecting these barriers are simply inflicting pain on themselves and those they purport to help.

REAL PEOPLE

Some of a program's mentees take longer to improve than others. A young man in our program struggled all the way from middle school to the first part of high school. Academically and athletically talented, he never seemed able to stay out of trouble, in or out of school. He argued with our program staff, fought fellow students, dropped out of programs we helped him get into, moved schools, disappeared.

Then one day in eleventh grade, he was back in the school we served—a new, focused young man. He attended our week of college search programming over the summer without incident. He was one of the few students we have who tackled the college application process with real determination, and got into the school he wanted to attend.

Resources

Adelman, C. (2006). *The toolbox revisited: Paths to degree completion from high school through college.* Washington, DC: US Department of Education.

Carnevale, A. & Rose, S. (2015). *The economy goes to college: The hidden promise of college in the post-industrial service economy.* Washington, DC: Georgetown University.

PART

What Is Mentoring?

What Does It Mean to Be a Mentor for Young People?

2

👥 REAL PEOPLE

Many years ago, when I was an unfocused undergraduate, the world-famous philosopher, Cornel West, showed me what a mentor is supposed to do.

A friend of mine, who looked up to West, was about to drop out of the university due to family financial crisis. I went to West's office hours, wedging myself in without an appointment, and told him the story. I asked for his help keeping her in school. Sitting at a desk covered in message slips for speaking engagements, West became upset at the thought of her withdrawal. "She is just beginning to live the life of the mind," he told me. "I'll go to the president for the money if I have to."

He jumped up, and told me to follow him to financial aid. We walked there together, and West lobbied the director of the office for extra help.

West acted as an exemplary mentor. He saw trouble on the horizon for his student and acted immediately to keep her in school. In that moment, even though I did not really understand what a mentor was, I understood that West had both the power to help people and the will to drop everything to do it. Being around West was like being on the court with Michael Jordan after he took a shot—you want to practice enough to become as good.

Mentoring: Then and Now

The noun and verb "mentor" date back to Homer's *Odyssey*. Mentoring in the *Odyssey* is born directly out of fatherlessness. Telemachus, the son and heir of King Odysseus, has no father to guide him: Odysseus left long ago for the Trojan War, and every day he does not return sinks the kingdom of Ithaca further into chaos. Odysseus's friend and advisor, named Mentor, an older man, steps into this situation to help guide Telemachus.

This absence of a father is something we think of more in modern society than the traditional society of the *Odyssey*. But on each page of the *Iliad* there are men dying in combat and in other misfortunes as they battle over Troy. The *Iliad*'s "sequel," the *Odyssey*, gives us a small taste of the impact. Like many in his generation, Odysseus is absent from his household, where he is needed to prevent the breakdown of his kingdom and to train his son for adulthood and leadership.

Mentoring in the *Odyssey* is born in violence and chaos. The Trojan War, a pointless series of invasions, attacks, siege, and pillaging, has destroyed the social order in the Mediterranean world. In Odysseus's absence, his home is terrorized by "suitors," fellow warriors who seek Penelope's hand in marriage. The traditional social order to peaceful courting has been upended by the violence of war, and the men who look for Penelope are more like home invaders than friendly visitors.

Telemachus, still a young man, is thrust into a situation he cannot handle alone or without guidance. He lacks the experience with violence to kill the invaders himself, or to muster the men of his homeland against them. He has not been instructed in ruling by his father, so he simply wavers in his plans.

 ## CONVERSATION STARTERS

— What does a good mentor do?

Many young people have an idea about mentoring, but may not be able to put their finger on what it is. They may think a mentor will do things for them, or make decisions on their behalf, rather than help them clarify their options.

What a Mentor Does

Mentor plays many roles in the *Odyssey*, both the human elder named Mentor, and the goddess Athena, who takes Mentor's form throughout the poem. These actions of Mentor inform what we today think of as mentoring.

Mentors Speak Up for Their Mentees

When Telemachus seeks help in his mission to learn about his father, people scorn him. Mentor speaks up for Telemachus, helping him achieve his mission. There are times when mentees just need someone to speak up on their behalf, often to save them from their own mistakes.

Mentors Challenge Their Mentees

When Telemachus needs guidance, Athena comes to him in the form of Mentor and tells him that, although sons are rarely as good as their fathers, Telemachus has the skills to begin his mission. Athena here seeks to challenge, not to soothe. While a human advisor might have reassured Telemachus, the divine Athena instead sets a high bar for him to aspire to. Mentoring young people is not just reassuring them, it is challenging them.

Mentors (Sometimes) Offer Direct Help

In the *Odyssey*, Mentor does more than advise; he actively organizes events so that Telemachus is successful in his mission. Athena, in the form of Mentor, rounds up a crew for Telemachus, gathers supplies, and finds a ship. In the *Odyssey*, mentoring can be very hands-on and matter of fact. Just as in real life, mentors may need to step in with some direct assistance.

This should be help that empowers young people, and assists them in taking on the task in the future. Individuals and mentoring programs need to make sure that they are building the capacity of the young people they mentor, not fighting every battle on their behalf. It should go without saying that loaning money to a mentee is a bad idea, though I have helped out with purchases or given graduation gifts instead.

Mentors Help Their Mentees Plan and to Implement the Plan

In the *Odyssey*, Mentor helps Telemachus get out of the house, and take steps to improve his and his family's situation. In modern terms, this may be getting someone off the couch, away from the videogames, out of the basement, and off to the world. Mentors often need to help mentees understand that they need a plan, and to help the mentee create his or her own plan.

Mentors Show That There Is a Plan

Mentors can also help mentees see a larger plan in their own lives. The very presence of Mentor at the side of Telemachus is read as a sign that the gods are on the young man's side—an important factor in swaying public opinion to Telemachus' side. In Greek society, whom the gods favor or disfavor would be an important piece of information for a person to make decisions about whom to follow. In modern life, we do not look for similar signs of divine favor, but mentors can reinforce the sense in the mentee that there is a plan, that great things are bound to happen if the correct route is followed and the wrong routes avoided.

Mentors Connect to the Spiritual as well as Material World

Working at a public institution funded by federal grants, I am always mindful that programming cannot be religious in content and that our participants have wide variation in spiritual practice, beliefs, and experience with religion. However, there is a religious/spiritual motivation to mentoring that goes beyond any social science outcomes. The beliefs that individuals can turn their lives around, that individuals who are lost can come back to the program, and that people can be redeemed, are all rooted in spiritual belief, though that can come from a wide variety of traditions.

This spiritual aspect of mentoring motivates people to have hope in situations that seem hopeless and to persevere in the face of the problems that seem insoluble. Over time, this hope is rewarding enough to keep mentors going in situations that, thought about in coldly rational terms, they would abandon. Without this sense of spiritual calling to mentoring, many participants would burn out or become discouraged.

 **REFLECTION**

— Who do you remember as an exemplary mentor? What did he or she do or say that made an impact?

Mentors Are Peacemakers and Mediators in the Lives of Young People

At the end of the *Odyssey*, after a bloodletting in Odysseus's palace, it is time for those involved in this bloodbath to figure out the next steps. Again, it is Athena, in the form of Mentor, who steps forward to close the narrative: "Then Minerva assumed the form and voice of Mentor, and presently made a covenant of peace between the two contending parties." This role of elders in making peace and bringing pointless conflicts to an end is needed more than ever.

 ## TIE TO LEADERSHIP

In what ways do you see mentoring throughout your program or organization? While many programs and buildings can deliver excellent services to young people, they often fall short in creating a culture of mentoring or making sure that all needs in the organization are being met. With lower funding levels throughout K–12 school districts and social-service organizations, there is a greater risk of burning out the people who work with young people, ending with either high-turnover organizations, or those where people stay on even though they are performing at a less-effective level.

In organizations that embrace servant leadership, laid out in the writings of Robert K. Greenleaf (1973), the whole leadership structure is inverted. The front-line people serve the participants, the supervisors support the front-line workers, and those at the top support everyone. This explicitly involves mentoring at all levels of the organization, so that people are able to reach their full potential in the organization. This is, perhaps, an impossible goal to reach, but a method that should be kept in mind in any organization, building, or program that purports to mentor.

Resources

Greenleaf, R. K. (1973). *The servant as leader* [rev.]. Cambridge, MA: Center for Applied Studies.

Homer (1990). *The Odyssey* [R. Fagles, trans.]. New York: Viking/Penguin.

3 | What Mentoring Can and Cannot Do

 **REAL PEOPLE**

After the Meeting

We had just wrapped up the meeting. One of our smartest, but most troubled, students had just turned down a place in an Early College program. This program would provide up to 60 free college credits and free books. His mother, a recent immigrant, had been unclear about the value of the program, and for the young man the lure of football and life in a big high school weighed more heavily on the scale than the Early College opportunity.

The meeting left my staff drained. Two staff members attended, advocating with the Early College about the student's potential, then advocating enrollment to the student and his mother. At the end of the meeting, the student decided against the program, despite years of intensive mentoring by two full-time staff.

We stood in front of our building, just crushed. One of us began to cry, and we all knew that we had just watched a serious setback in the life of a young man. This kind of moment, familiar to people who run mentoring programs, is important, because it shows us the limits of what we can accomplish.

When thinking about mentoring, sometimes I envision a young person's life in the balance on a scale, with the weight of hope on one side and the barriers on the other. I find myself putting out a finger to place on the side of hope, hoping that this small weight will tip the balance.

This helps me keep in mind that, at times, mentoring is enough to move a young person in a positive direction. But at other times, multiple factors—the weight of violence and the neighborhood environment, young people's own poor judgment, immaturity, and pure stubbornness—just push down too hard, leaving even multiple mentors feeling powerless and cast aside.

The Discovery of Mentoring

Between the time *Odyssey* was written and the 1970s, mentoring has had a steady but unglamorous history. Used as a term for coaching or advising, the word "mentor" was used in the title of advice manuals and other books intended to give ambitious young men a leg up on their courtly and business careers. By the twentieth century, mentor was a synonym for coach, used in college football as an almost informal verb, as in "he mentored at Cornell." From college coaching, the term made its way into the college classroom, as "mentor" became a synonym for a college professor in the latter half of the twentieth century.

As a high-profile concept, mentoring arrived in 1978 as part of the literature on business leadership. In the late 1970s, an age of economic slowdown and political "malaise" in America, mentoring seemed a way forward for both individuals and social institutions. The article that put the concept of mentoring on the map in business was Collins and Scott (1978), "Everyone who makes it has a mentor," published in *Harvard Business Review*. This article, a collection of interviews with top business leaders, made the case that good mentoring was the key to reaching the very top of the corporate ladder.

The article, and the concept of corporate mentoring, was not uncontroversial. The publication of the article led to some backlash among other writers, particularly women, as the evidence base of the article—the experience of four elderly white males—was so narrow as to draw fire from those who pointed out that not all who got ahead had an official "mentor," and that not everyone who had a mentor had risen to the same level as the four men profiled.

From business, the concept of mentoring and its critical importance made its way into education in the 1980s and 1990s, now applied to helping young people make it to college. Arthur Levine and Jana Nidiffer's 1995 book, *Beating the odds: How the poor get to college*, looked at the factors that bring low-income students to college and had findings similar to Collins and Scott. After interviewing high-performing, low-income students who successfully make the jump to college, they found that a single individual could make a world of difference for a young person, making him or her believe in the dream of college and a better life. No one in their study "made it" without this type of mentoring intervention.

 **REFLECTION**

> —Was there a mentor in your own life who was your "beating the odds" adult? What did this person do to offer the encouragement you needed at the time?

These arguments are powerful, and they connect to many people's personal experiences. Readers can remember figures in their lives who have believed in them and encouraged them to take on challenges that seemed daunting at the time. But this type of research is not conclusive. It measures successful people and then looks for what they have in common, without ever examining the experiences of the unsuccessful. This does not make this research wrong, but it should lead us to ask broader questions about mentoring.

Throughout the 1970s and 1980s, research and writing about young people in poverty pointed to mentoring as a key strategy to help young people. The books *Tough change: Growing up on your own in America* (Lefkowitz, 1987) and *Growing up poor* (Williams & Kornblum, 1985) both pointed to adults, unrelated to the young people they mentored, as keys that allowed young people in poor neighborhoods to find opportunities. Unfortunately, in many cases these opportunities were reserved for top athletes in high schools, mentored by local boosters who hoped to aid their alma mater with a top recruit. Broader or more systematic attempts to reach young people did not exist in these neighborhoods, and little effort was made to aid those with academic potential.

The study of mentoring took a quantum leap in sophistication when Jean Rhodes's (2002) book, *Stand by me: The risks and rewards of mentoring today's youth*, examined the research literature on mentoring that drew from a wider pool of subjects. Rather than looking at 4 or 20 subjects, this quantitative study examined more than 1,000 young people who had participated in Big Brothers/Big Sisters (a youth mentoring program which pairs up young people—"Littles"—with older adults—"Bigs"—for one-on-one activities over a period of years) in order to evaluate the effectiveness of the largest, best-run program of its type in the nation. The effect size of mentoring programs was smaller than might have been expected: approximately .05 (i.e., very small).

Rhodes (2002) does point to three positive mentoring outcomes: enhancing social skills and emotional well-being, improving cognitive skills through dialogue and listening, and serving as a role model and advocate. However, she presents the negative potential of mentoring as well. When adults are inconsistent in their mentoring efforts, the young people involved suffer harm, more than they would had they merely been left alone. The impact of early termination (fewer than six months) was seen in areas such as perception of competence, school attendance, pro-social behavior, and abstinence. The highest benefits of mentoring were seen in relationships that lasted more than a year.

Much of the benefit in mentoring came from setting up good matches. Rhodes developed a survey to measure how well a mentoring relationship was working, covering four major areas:

- Is the relationship helpful?
- Does it meet expectations?
- Does it evoke negative emotions?
- Does the protégé feel close to the mentor?

The absence of negative feeling, Rhodes noted, was a more important predictor of mentoring success than statements of happiness with the mentoring relationship.

 ## CONVERSATION STARTERS

— What do you expect out of the relationship as a mentee?

Sometimes young people have unrealistic ideas of a mentor's omnipotence. It can be productive to just talk about what a mentor does, and how it is different than a teacher, counselor, friend, or superhero.

TIE TO LEADERSHIP

How Researchers Understand Mentoring

David DuBois and colleagues completed a meta-analysis of programs for youth in 2002, finding 55 studies of mentoring to examine. A meta-analysis can tell you, based on a multitude of studies, whether a type of program has an impact on young people, and what the approximate size of that impact is. For youth mentoring programs, this program impact was small, but those programs that were based on research and evidence had a higher impact than those that did not. Programs in schools had less of an impact than those based in the workplace or the community. Matching the race, gender, or interests of mentors and mentees had no impact. Programs with a moderator to help facilitate programming and those that utilized mentors in helping professions (e.g., teaching) scored higher, as did programs with more intensity (more than two hours a week) and with longer duration (more than one year).

A follow-up study of one-on-one mentoring in 2008 found that academic, workplace, and youth mentoring all had positive impacts, and measured these at higher levels than the earlier study. Mentoring that includes academics was found to be most effective, workplace mentoring next, and generic youth mentoring third but still showing a positive impact (Eby, 2008).

The research on mentoring programs should raise some issues for even the most committed proponent of mentoring. Even the largest, best-run programs simply do not generate the kinds of results we would like to see. Programs do not manage to halt the slide, academic and personal, that afflicts most teenage participants. What programs can accomplish is often simply to change the slope of that decline, relative to what it would be in the absence of mentoring.

So what message does research have for mentors?

1. **Go forth and mentor . . .** Research shows us that consistent mentoring has a positive impact, even if that impact is not documented to be as great as we would hope it to be. In real life, we need to decide if mentoring is better than leaving young people entirely to their own devices. So if

mentoring is part of a solid program, with a long-term commitment to young people, research tells us to move forward and make the effort on their behalf.

2. **. . . But only if it is backed by commitment.** Poorly conceived, drive-by programs are proven by research to have a negligible or even negative outcome.

3. **Don't believe the hype.** Mentoring programs cannot positively change all youth outcomes by themselves. Schools need to perform better, health-care systems need to improve their interactions with young people, and mental-health services need to be more broadly available. All of this needs to happen for young people to flourish.

4. **Be encouraged.** Mentors do make a difference, albeit not as big a difference as one would hope, and sometimes just a difference in reducing the level of bad outcomes that young people experience in their teen years. Even when what young people are experiencing is quite bad, ask yourself if it would be better for them to go through the situation alone, or with at least one adult who cares about how the situation turns out?

 **REFLECTION**

— How do you know your program or a proposed program is effective?
— What key measures do you use now, or would you like to add?

Resources

Collins, E. G., & Scott, P. (1978) "'Everyone who makes it has a mentor:' Interviews with F. J. Lunding, G. E. Clements, and D. S. Perkins." *Harvard Business Review*, July–August, p. 89.

DuBois, D. L., Holloway, B. E., Valentine, J. C., & Cooper, H. (2002). "Effectiveness of mentoring programs for youth: A meta-analytic review." *American Journal of Community Psychology*, 30:2, 157–197.

Eby, L. T., Allen, T. D., Evans, S. C., Ng, T., & DuBois, D. (2008). "Does mentoring matter? A multidisciplinary meta-analysis comparing mentored and non-mentored individuals." *Journal of Vocational Behavior*, 72:2, 254–267.

Lefkowitz, B. (1987). *Tough change: Growing up on your own in America.* New York: Free Press.

Levine, A., & Nidiffer, J. (1995). *Beating the odds: How the poor get to college.* San Francisco: Jossey-Bass.

Rhodes, J. E. (2002). *Stand by me: The risks and rewards of mentoring today's youth.* Cambridge, MA: Harvard University Press.

Rhodes, J. E. and DuBois, D. L. (2008). "Mentoring relationships and programs for youth." *Current Directions in Psychological Science.* http://friendsof thechildren.org/wp-content/uploads/2010/01/Mentoring-Relationships-Programs-for-Youth.pdf

Williams, T. M., & Kornblum, W. (1985). *Growing up poor.* Lexington, MA: Lexington Books.

Setting Up Programs and Relationships the Right Way

 **REAL PEOPLE**

I had agreed to work with an undergraduate on a project where we would travel to a local school for a few sessions to do literacy activities with third-grade students. My partner in this endeavor was an African-American young man, and I thought nothing about how the third graders would react to us. When we showed up to class, I quickly realized that he was the star, especially with African-American boys. Boys would line up to be read to by him. Even though I had taught literacy classes and had experience working in the schools, there was an almost gravitational attraction of the boys in class to this young man. Luckily, he was incredibly responsible and made it back to the class several times to read and interact with the class. (He walked to the school once when I was unable to go.) These African-American boys craved this young man's attention and presence in a way that they did not with me, a middle-aged white man.

What Makes a Good Mentor?

We know a lot more about what does not matter for mentors and mentees than what really does matter. Having mentors who are the same race and gender as the mentees you serve can be ideal, especially in the view of parents (Liang & West, 2007). But researchers have found programs that have cross-race or cross-gender pairs that are effective as well (Rhodes, 2002). Programs that create one-to-one paired mentor relationships are constantly recruiting for men of color to serve as mentors, but there are almost never enough to cover the need. Group mentoring provides more flexibility and also allows mentors to cover multiple sites to work with many participants.

While the demographics of the mentor are important, I have seen relationships grow in unlikely ways. By high school, many students want to connect with someone in their desired career field and will gravitate to adults based on their aspirations more than on background alone. There are individuals who are skilled at working with young people who are not what they are, and prefer to work across class/race/gender lines with mentees. There are also solid programmatic reasons to mix pairs. Mentoring programs exist to offer services, not build wait lists. The sooner each young person in your program is paired, the sooner each one may see benefit from the program.

Research shows that for mentoring programs, mentors need to be engaged and committed in order to have a positive impact. When looking for mentors, that variable is more important than career success, charisma, fun, education, or sports ability. Young people, for all their problems, have unbelievably good dishonesty detectors, and can quickly figure out which adults are going to take them seriously and keep their promises.

What to Look for in a Potential Mentor

- **Responsibility**: mentors need to be reliable for the relationship to be positive. Folks who have trouble making it from one place to another on time should be steered to a less demanding form of community service.
- **Caring**: mentors should be able to explain why they care about young people and what that means to them. This should not be related to a need for friendship or romance. It needs to be driven by the right motivations for entering into a mentoring relationship.
- **Boundaries and rules**: mentors need to have a strong sense of what they should and should not do as mentors. They should understand the rules that the mentoring program sets for mentor–mentee relationships and understand the importance of keeping those rules. People who show a cavalier attitude towards rules in general are not a good fit for youth programs.
- **Personal history of mentoring or needing help**: folks who have lived sheltered or charmed lives make bad mentors as they have little real experience in dealing with the issues that their mentees face. Much like the "A" student trying to tutor math, people who are too successful really cannot explain how to get to where they are. People who have faced

problems, overcome them, and can explain how they did it are the best fit for mentoring.

- **Grit**: people who embrace challenge and hard work are good role models for young people. This does not mean that they are just plain hard-headed, but that they have set goals for themselves, worked hard, overcome defeat, and gone on to success. Grit also means that people have passion about their goals, the kind of enthusiasm that can help light up activities and discussions.

- **Growth mindset**: mentors need to believe that mentees and their situations can improve. Adults who cannot see potential for change and growth are not going to do young people any good. Young people have encountered enough other adults who do not believe in their potential. Mentors need to work against this dynamic, not feed it.

- **Admitting mistakes and learning from failure**: mentors need to be able to own their mistakes and failures, and learn from them. We are often teaching young people to "fail forward," so the adults involved in the program need to be comfortable with learning from their missteps.

- **Having their stuff together**: mentors need to be functioning, relatively successful adults. They do not need to be millionaires, but some success in the workplace is helpful as a mentor. They do not need to be the mom or dad on a 1950s sitcom, but some stability and happiness in their personal life is important. Mentors need to live less volatile lives than their mentees. At moments, we have had to have people step out of the mentoring program for a short time to deal with personal issues, modeling responsible adult behavior.

REFLECTION

— What successes in life do you bring to the mentoring relationship? What issues are you still working on?

— Entering a mentoring program or relationship can challenge you to build your skill set and can have an impact on your career, as well as that of your mentee.

Musts to Avoid

People who come to mentoring programs to fill a void in their own lives are an absolute must to avoid. We have had incidents of people using youth programs as a way to seek friends or romantic partners, at times without meaning to do so. Without being uncompassionate, mentoring programs need to be very clear that mentoring is not a source of friendship or dates for mentors. Mentors and mentees should not have contact outside of program policy, including electronic or social-media contact.

People who are not good about keeping to rules are often a bad risk for programs. People who are trusted to work with young people need to understand the risks for programs of sexual abuse, and need to be willing to commit to policies to prevent abuse, such as not touching their mentees. Individuals who seem disinclined to follow small rules in life are often at risk of going astray with larger ones. Since mentoring programs teach young people about the need to take responsibility for one's actions, adults who seem to shirk their responsibilities are not going to provide the modeling needed.

Powerful Pairs and Groups

There is no right way to pair young people with mentors. While pairing by race and gender is more common, it is not required. Setting pairs by interest or background can also yield powerful relationships. Programs that work hard to pair young people appropriately spend a good deal of time thinking about pairs ahead of time, then also spend effort monitoring the pairs and making sure that the relationship is engaging to both the mentor and mentee.

Group mentoring offers more options as you are then building a team. This means that not every mentor needs to have every positive characteristic. This can open up the possibility of having mentors at very different stages of their careers, as well as very different stages of their lives. Our teams have included special educators, ministers, social workers, athletes, professors, after-school staff, graduate students, and cooks. Group mentoring gives young people the option of meeting a range of adults, giving them a chance to connect with one more strongly than another if that is desired.

Having students mentored by more than one person also allows for the ebb and flow of mentoring relationships to occur without damage. If a student receives a difficult message from one adult in the program, she or he can disengage temporarily. But if the student has more than one point of contact with the program, the mentoring can continue until the original relationship can be repaired.

There is nothing wrong with asking young people their preferences, though at times they may prefer a group just to be less conspicuous. A combination of the two (large group for a speaker, then break into pairs) can also be effective.

CONVERSATION STARTERS

— Would you rather work with a mentor one-on-one or in a group?

Screening, Interviewing, and Supervising

Screening

No one ever started a mentoring program in order to do background searches for potential mentors. Screening for criminal background is a difficult issue, as many individuals who would be great mentors have had significant trouble in their lives in the past. While this enables them to connect with young people on a different level than other adults, mentoring programs need to be smart about screening.

At our office, we run all staff and volunteers (me included) through a computerized background check that we can do from our offices. This gives us evidence of involvement with crimes against children and young people. There is another database for crimes reported within the state, and for employees we run a full FBI fingerprint check.

We always tell potential employees and volunteers that we do this, but we first ask whether we can expect anything from the system. This is a key moment. People who are upfront about their past, and take responsibility for what happened, stand out here as positive role models. Folks who let us discover their past mistakes ourselves often become far less desirable candidates as a result. Often, young people do not really see their involvement in such crimes as drug possession, even assault, as a "big deal," and try to minimize its importance. A more important predictor of success as a mentor is how people talk about their past, not what they did. Adults with serious crimes on their records that happened a decade ago are a much better risk than younger people who have had trouble in their very recent past. There are people in our community who, in spite of multiple felonies, are respected mentors in their neighborhoods.

While uncomfortable conversations to have, background-check discussions, if handled with dignity, can help one learn a lot about an adult's background, and help the potential mentor learn about the program's values. Openly discussing issues of criminal background can also help people learn more about programs such as expungement, which can help adults remove their juvenile criminal problems from their records with the help of the courts.

Interviewing

When talking to potential mentors, it is good to be upfront about the goals of your program and your expectations of mentors. The following questions work well with potential mentors:

- What were some of the problems you faced in middle and high school?
- What adults helped you navigate problems when you were that age?
- Who are mentors in your life now?
- What drew you to work with young people?
- How do you know when to give advice?
- What are you passionate about?
- What experience have you had working with youth?
- How can this experience help your career?

The answers to the questions above can be many and different, but the conversation should show that the applicant has reflected on his or her experience, demonstrating maturity and depth of commitment. People who offer canned responses, or who do not show that they have reflected and grown from their experiences, may not be a good fit for the program.

Training/Supervising

I am a big supporter of mentor training, and I try to be present at as many sessions as I can. Prospective mentors need at least an hour of training, including program policies, legal issues, the proper role of a mentor, and the importance of responsibility in a mentoring relationship. We often include some case studies for participants to talk about, and I try to draw on their own experiences in the training.

Having a check-in with mentors is essential. In a group program, this can be a meeting between sessions to troubleshoot. With matched pair programs, a phone call or email check-in can help ensure that things are going well for both mentor and mentee. The ability of a program to keep track of both youth and adults is the key to creating the engagement needed. Pairs can fall apart easily if the young person changes residences or schools, so programs need to be nimble about tracking the comings and goings of the mentees.

 REAL PEOPLE

Am I Setting a Good Example?

When I lived in Cambridge, Massachusetts, I took on a student to tutor in chemistry at the local high school. As a graduate student, I was unfocused in my use of time, and my tutee was not always showing up for sessions to meet with me. Plus, chemistry is a hard subject, and I needed to read up to even help out at all.

One day, I just did not show up for a session. The program policy was to have a program staff dial my number, then hand the high school student the phone. He left a message on my machine about my absence. When I got it I was mortified. That call changed the way I thought about mentoring, and it finally made me realize the level of disappointment I had caused by my absence.

When to End a Volunteer's Involvement in Mentoring

Terminating volunteers' involvement is always awkward. Since people are donating their time, it seems mean-spirited to let them go. But finding a way to end unproductive relationships is one of the keys to maintaining a high-quality program. If mentors are unreliable, if discussions seem really off topic, if joking around seems to go too far, or if program boundaries are not being fully respected, it is time to let the adult mentor go and reassign the young person. If a young person is disruptive enough to a program, he or she may also need to be let go, as a last resort. Over time, good programs convey the lesson that mentoring relationships that are drifting do not right themselves on their own, and some intervention may be needed, which could include reassigning the youth to a new mentor.

TIE TO LEADERSHIP

Motivational Interviewing

How can you get young people to move from where they are to where they want to be? Psychologists William Miller and Stephen Rollnick have developed "motivational interviewing" as one method of connecting to their patients, including young people. In order for motivational interviewing to be a success, the following conditions must be met:

- The two people involved must be committed to the relationship.
- The mentee needs to feel unhappy with the area under discussion— the mentor must feel confident in this area of life.
- The mentor must be able to offer empathy and encouragement to the mentee, and must be able to put her or himself in the shoes of the mentee.
- The mentor can then help the mentee identify the gaps between the present situation and the mentee's goal, and help the mentee identify the strengths he or she has in this area, to build a greater sense of self-efficacy.

Resources

Centers for Disease Control and Prevention. "Preventing child sexual abuse within youth-serving organizations: Getting started on policies and procedures." www.cdc.gov/ViolencePrevention/pub/PreventingChild Abuse.html

Corporation for National & Community Service. *Toolkit: National Mentoring Month.* www.nationalservice.gov/pdf/06_1220_nmm_toolkit.pdf

Duckworth, A. L. (2013). "The key to success? Grit." www.ted.com/speakers/ angela_lee_duckworth

Dweck, C. S. (2006). *Mindset: The new psychology of success.* New York: Random House.

Dweck, C. S. (2014). "The power of believing that you can improve." www. ted.com/speakers/carol_dweck

Liang, B., & West, J. (2007). *Youth mentoring: Do race and ethnicity really matter?* Alexandria, VA: National Mentoring Partnership. www. mentoring.org/downloads/mentoring_390.pdf

Rhodes, J. (2002). *Research corner: Mentoring and race.* Alexandria, VA: National Mentoring Partnership. www.mentoring.org/downloads/mentoring_1320.pdf

Tough, P. (2012). *How children succeed: Grit, curiosity, and the hidden power of character.* Boston, MA: Houghton Mifflin Harcourt.

The website www.mentoring.org provides resources for programs, including a publication *Elements of effective practice for mentoring.*

5 | Barriers and Limits to Mentoring

 **REAL PEOPLE**

A Dilemma

Mentoring programs always need money. A company approached our Young Men's Leadership Program about sponsoring some students to go through a mentoring program. The catch was that the organization was part of the medical marijuana industry. While appreciating the civic gesture, we knew that the young men we were working with did not need any more exposure to or encouragement to use marijuana.

Trouble that Young People Get Into

Young people make mistakes that vastly influence their futures. From risk taking behind the wheel of an automobile, to engaging in sexual relationships that they are unprepared to handle, to failing to turn in homework, to committing petty crimes that have long-term consequences, young people are far less likely than adults to understand the risks they take, and are often unprepared to face the consequences. In middle- and upper-class families, parents and others can often intervene and make problems "go away," but in working-class and poor families, the teens are often facing the negative consequences on their own.

⬡ REFLECTION

— What was the worst kind of trouble you got into as an adolescent?
— How was it handled by your parents and those in authority?
— How might the situation have played out differently, and reshaped your life?

Young People and Crime

While juvenile crime is down in America, young people are still being arrested each day for a wide variety of offenses. In 1980, juvenile arrests were at 6 per 100 young people, and they are now closer to 4 per 100 (OJJDP, 2013). Of the 1.3 million juvenile arrests in 2012, 71 percent were for young men, 72 percent were for those older than 15, and 35 percent of those arrested were non-white. Most arrests were for minor property crimes, such as shoplifting, with the other major categories for youth including assault, drug offenses, and disorderly conduct. Once they get involved in the criminal justice system, it is often hard for young people to get out. A single arrest can put young people into the juvenile court system, and then subsequent offenses can get them shifted into adult court, with the potential for adult prison.

Many juvenile courts have turned to mentoring as a strategy to keep children out of the system when they first make contact with law enforcement. These diversion programs pair up young offenders with a mentor, often a college student, to build a pro-social bond with a caring adult. For many young people, this relationship can make all the difference. For young people in the diversion program in my county (Washtenaw County in Michigan), paired with Eastern Michigan University social work students, the recidivism rate is only 8 percent, with more young people going on to adulthood without an adult criminal record.

👥 REAL PEOPLE

Jennifer Kellman-Fritz and Deborah Shaw have developed mentoring programs to help keep young people who get into contact with the law from continuing along this path. Jennifer runs a mentoring program with EMU students in social work, and Debbie connects the program to the juvenile court system. Funded by some small grants, they have helped dozens of young people get out of the pipeline, graduate from high school, and move on with their adult lives.

The Youth Risk Behavior Surveillance System

If you want a quick look at the problems you are up against as a mentor, the Youth Risk Behavior Surveillance System (YRBSS) is a great place to start. This survey examines the risks that students are taking nation-wide, and gives a good snapshot of what students are up to when they are out of your sightline. I often show results of the survey of teens to prospective teachers, who often react in shock that young people are engaged in any negative behaviors outside the classroom.

The data that follows in this chapter is drawn from this survey's results. Even if the statistics do not apply to the student you are personally mentoring, it is a good reflection of what is surrounding that young person, and what he or she is seeing or hearing about in the hall between classes, in the locker room, or being texted about on the phone.

Tobacco, Alcohol, and Drugs

First, the good news. For those of us raised at a time when most young people tried cigarettes, teens today just do not smoke tobacco very much at all. As schools have eliminated smoking areas and lounges for students and faculty, smoking has become less cool. Only a small minority (about 6 percent) of students smoke cigarettes regularly, with slightly greater percentages using smokeless tobacco (8 percent) or cigarillos (13 percent).

The bad news is that while cigarette use has dropped, use of other drugs has increased. Over a third (35 percent) of teens use alcohol. Two-fifths (40 percent) have tried marijuana and almost a quarter (23 percent) use it currently. The other drugs we think of as "hard drugs" are all under 10 percent, but use of others' prescription medication is at 18 percent of teens.

For me growing up, I saw alcohol and tobacco as the main outlets for teenagers, with a smaller group moving on to marijuana or other drugs. This has shifted with this generation, as marijuana has become more available and its image has changed. Unfortunately, marijuana has a disproportionate impact on the developing brains of teens (American Psychological Association, 2014).

Sexual Activity, Identity, and Pregnancy

By ninth grade, almost a third (30 percent) of students have had sex at least once, and by senior year, this proportion increases to a majority of students (64 percent). By the end of high school, almost half (49 percent) of students are regularly sexually active. Many young people are not taking precautions about the consequences of this activity: less than half (41 percent) are not always using condoms, and the vast majority of women (81 percent) are not using birth control pills. While there can be many reasons for this lack of preparation, the bottom line is that mentors and mentoring programs should not assume that young people are abstinent, nor that they know and are able to be involved in what adults would consider a sexually responsible and safe relationship.

For teens who identify as lesbian, gay, or bisexual, publicly coming out to their family or school may put them at risk. The age at which young people declare their identity to friends and family, often at school, has declined from the 18–22 range, with an average now around 16. This can put these young people at higher risk of bullying and being cut off by their family. As the age of coming out has become younger, those young people are more vulnerable to poor treatment at the hands of peers and family, and have fewer resources to defend themselves. However, the peer climate at many schools has shifted in positive directions, as many more schools have "Gay–Straight Alliances" that help create a safe, positive environment for students. A decade ago, this level of peer support would be considered remarkable, while now it is closer to the norm.

More students are also identifying as differently gendered—sometimes transgendered (a boy who identifies as a girl, or *vice versa*) or young people who locate themselves outside the two-gender system. These expressions can put some young people in real danger of harassment and bullying, and caring adults are really needed to help nurture these young people no matter their gender expression. For adult mentors, dealing with students with different ideas about sexuality and gender than their own can be disconcerting. This is a case where reassigning a mentor to find someone more comfortable and familiar with the issues teens face right now would be better.

For teens, parenthood is often the event that stops their education career or puts it on hold. Whether in high school or early in college, becoming a parent means more responsibility than many students can handle, and many young people drop out of school to work or take care of the child. While in many cases this is admirable, taking up the responsibility to be a mother or father at a young age, it often means dropping out of college, returning home, and taking an entry-level job, often after racking up bills and loans for an education that is not yet complete.

Just Plain Risks

Young people are at greater danger from a variety of sources, sometimes due to their behavior and age. Most (88 percent) will not wear a bicycle helmet consistently, some (10 percent) report that they have driven under the influence of alcohol, and a greater proportion (21 percent) indicate they have driven with someone who was under the influence. Two-fifths (40 percent) report they text while driving.

Young people, particularly in urban schools, face other issues as well, many stemming from personal safety and the availability of weapons. In surveys, almost a sizable minority (18 percent) of students report that they have carried a weapon (gun or knife) for protection. Almost one-quarter (20 percent) of girls and nearly one-third (30 percent) of boys indicated that they were in a physical fight in the past year, and many report being electronically bullied (21 percent of girls and 9 percent of boys). Girls are more likely than boys to feel bullied, on or off school property.

There is only so much any adult can do to help alter the above statistics. At the least, mentors can model responsible behavior, encourage being safe, and genuinely support young people when they face harassment and bullying. Young people can be surprisingly resilient in the face of pressure and poor treatment from their peers, if the adults in their lives support them 100 percent. Mentors can also support young people when they stick up for one another in the face of in-person or online harassment—this can help create a better environment for youth, on and offline.

Mental Health

The teen years are tough ones for mental health, with many mental illnesses having an initial onset period during the adolescent years. About a third (30 percent) of all young people report feeling sad or hopeless (39 percent of girls, 21 percent of boys). Some have considered suicide (22 percent of girls and 11 percent of boys). A smaller group of young people plan suicide (14 percent), make an attempt (8 percent), or seek treatment as a result of an attempt (3 percent), but this issue is an important one for mentoring programs to keep in mind and be prepared for. The stigma that is attached to seeking mental-health counseling is still high, particularly in low-income communities, and programs should seek out partners who provide this care in a way that can gently get youth and families the help they need.

Young people can also grapple with grief as a mental-health issue. Due to their family and neighborhood circumstance, many low-income students are dealing with levels of death and mortality that usually show up for middle-class children much later in life. While a middle-class student may grapple with the loss of a grandparent while in college, a low-income student may lose a parent while in high school, a greater loss at a much younger age. Finding ways to help students acknowledge loss, and providing groups or resources to help them grieve, is a key area where mentors and mentoring programs can help young people make this passage in a healthy manner.

CONVERSATION STARTERS

— In the past month, have you been bothered by feeling down, depressed, or hopeless? Have you been bothered by little interest or pleasure in doing things?

These two questions are a validated depression screening tool you can use to find out if a mentee needs further attention from a counselor.

The Teenage Brain as a Barrier

Cognitive science has shown that young people have a brain that is not wired for the adolescence that we provide for them. As teenagers, young people are pushed out of bed hours before they are at their best, they are bussed to high schools that often fail to challenge or engage their brain, they are surrounded by peers who can be a bad influence on their thinking, and they are kept busy enough so that they lack the sleep they need. Added to this, at a time in life when the brain is least able to make good long-term judgments, and is more likely to grasp at quick, peer-influenced rewards, we ask teens to make some of the most fateful educational and career decisions of their lives.

This does not mean that it is impossible for teens to make good, pro-social, thoughtful, long-term decisions. However, the odds are certainly against it, and teens need support. Making a decision about college or other post-secondary options while aged 18 is like taking up a sport or other physical activity as a middle-aged person: it can be done, it can be valuable, but you are fighting nature every step of the way.

Lawrence Steinberg's (2014) research has shown that teens are not necessarily terrible decision-makers, but they can be influenced in ways that can be very negative. Teens make more impulsive decisions when their peers are present, and they take more risks than when adults are present. But this influence can cut two ways: they are also open to more pro-social messages from their peers.

In building mentoring relationships and programs, these findings should give us some hope. If we can surround teens with some positive adults, their presence alone could head off some poor decisions, just because of their proximity and influence. If we can add to that building pro-social groups of young people who can positively influence one another, this can head off many of the problems we worry about for our teens.

TIE TO LEADERSHIP

When you are looking at program or school rules, can you find ways to steer students clear of risks, or to help them recover when they stumble? For many schools, particularly those in urban areas, school discipline is the first step in a chain of events that can often lead, over time, to prison. As students move from suspension, to expulsion, to juvenile crime, to being charged as an adult, they are rarely able to get the fresh start that they may need to change their paths. The system itself makes this difficult, sometimes sweeping students along like a rapids, each mistake leading to more dangerous consequences.

When dealing with students and mentees, are there ways to help them make a fresh start? Some mentoring programs are part of diversion processes, in which students who have had contact with the criminal justice system or school disciplinary processes receive mentoring to help them get back on track. This can include meeting with a mentor, attending workshops, and activities to get youth out of their neighborhood and neighborhood school to see the wider world.

Programs such as restorative justice have also helped youth move from risky behavior to smarter choices. If young people who have broken the rules get to understand the harm and pain they have caused, and have an opportunity to make amends, they can become more empathetic and begin to make better choices. Building programs that help youth understand the long-term consequences of their actions can help get them to steer away from behavior that will not help them reach their goals. Progress on this can be slow, but over time these good decisions can become good habits and lead to greater success.

 REAL PEOPLE

When we asked one young man what he had really learned as a result of our program, he told us that his friends asked him to smoke pot, and he declined. Mentoring is not an immunization against unwise behavior, but all programs have to savor even the small victories of getting young people to make the right decision.

Resources

American Psychological Association (2014). "Regular marijuana use bad for teens' brains." www.apa.org/news/press/releases/2014/08/regular-marijuana.aspx

Human Rights Campaign. *Growing up LGBT in America.* www.hrc.org/files/assets/resources/Growing-Up-LGBT-in-America_Report.pdf

OJJDP (Office of Juvenile Justice and Delinquency Prevention) (2013). *Statistical Briefing Book.* Washington, DC: author. www.ojjdp.gov/ojstatbb/crime

Steinberg, L. D. (2014). *Age of opportunity: Lessons from the new science of adolescence.* Boston, MA: Houghton Mifflin Harcourt.

Data from the Youth Risk Behavior Surveillance System is available at www.cdc.gov/healthyyouth/data/yrbs/index.htm

6

Starting at "Ground Zero"

The Issues Young Men Face

Problems and Barriers

Of all groups in middle and high school, young men, particularly young men of color, face the highest barriers and enjoy the fewest supports. While in many high schools there will be some young men at the top of their class academically, or top male athletes, there are many more young men who are disconnected from academics and uninvolved with any activity. Many young men graduate without distinction from high school, or drop out of school to work, or simply disappear one day into the street. How we address the needs of these young men will define the next generation, because they could go either way. They could become great engineers, businesspeople, health-care providers, husbands or partners, fathers, and community members, or they could end up trapped in the criminal justice system.

 **REAL PEOPLE**

Alejandro Baldwin was working as a paraprofessional with emotionally impaired students when he realized that he wanted to work to help young men in his community. He developed the DAVID curriculum—Developing Accountability, Vision, Integrity, and Discipline—to help connect young men to their own community. In this model, young people need to assess their lives for "giants"—the things internally or externally that hold them back—and then find a way to address these. Then young men make a plan to change the situation for the better: for themselves, for their family, for their neighborhood. As Alejandro always tells young men: "If no one is doing something about an issue, that means you need to step up and address it." Baldwin implemented the program through

EMU's GEAR UP program, then brought the program with him to the University of Michigan, and now to his new home in Philadelphia.

Bad Image

Young men, as a group, have a bad reputation. At an early age, they can be labeled as trouble-makers, and that label is easy to get and difficult to lose. As Pierre Rice, who has worked with our Young Men's Leadership Program, told me, the students in his program are labeled by teachers as trouble-makers as early as second grade, and elementary teachers can become afraid of these students early in their academic careers. This causes a cycle of problems as the boys themselves learn that adults are frightened of them—and act accordingly. By middle school, boys can already feel that they are bad, and that adults are scared of them. This is a toxic combination.

By middle school, young men are in an impossible situation. They feel that they must keep up an image of toughness, even when this image does not help them at school. Boys tend to form themselves into hierarchies, top to bottom in terms of toughness and resourcefulness, through challenging each other verbally and physically. As Geoffrey Canada (1995) notes in his book, *Fist, stick, knife, gun*, when elementary schools feed into larger middle schools, each boy must re-prove himself, leading to wide-ranging violence as students enter larger schools. When students reach high school, the same pattern occurs, but often in more dangerous ways, as gangs and weapons become more a part of youth lives. This pattern also occurs when policy makers decide to consolidate urban secondary schools. City after city has closed schools and merged populations into high schools, cutting across neighborhood and gang lines, leading to a predictable spike of violence.

As Pierre Rice told me, at the high school level, young men must appear tough and ready to fight to help ward off the trouble that would inevitably occur if they were perceived as weak. Even if young men want to walk away from a confrontation, or not watch someone else's confrontation, young men are forced to stick to the script that they are tough and ready to fight. So young men who would just as soon stay clear of trouble will be at a fight with their cell phone out taking video, even if this puts them in harm's way. But a whole school of young men on edge and ready to fight is not a safe place. The stress of knowing that violence can break out at any time, and that adults will not be able to protect you, wears on young men. It decreases their focus on anything else in their lives.

Worst of all, adults prey on young men and boys, expanding and escalating conflicts quickly. Gangs are an adult enterprise, often managed by men who have graduated from the state prison system. These informal groupings recruit middle and high school young men as entry-level members, and as a result, a conflict between two young men can end with adults showing up to a school with weapons to settle the matter. Family and extended family relationships can also draw young men into conflicts that otherwise might die down. Social media are gasoline for the fire, with photos posted of young men holding weapons, an implicit threat to others.

All of these threats are self-fulfilling prophesies. In many cases, it is just a matter of time before conflicts between young men become neighborhood, family, or gang conflicts, often arising from moving schools or changing neighborhoods. As John Rich (2009) wrote in his book, *Wrong place, wrong time: Trauma and violence in the lives of young black men*, we must create an environment where everyone feels safe. This applies even to the students and community members whom people might feel initially scared of, or who seem threatening to others. Until all students feel that they are in a safe environment, they are not going to be able to let down their guard at all.

 **REFLECTION**

— What was the image that young men aspired to where you grew up?
— What behaviors were expected from them?
— How did this affect how their lives turned out over the long term?

Mentoring: Best and Worst of Times

Despite (or due to) the above challenges, young men cry out for mentoring and for programs to help them be more successful. The programs we have run for young men's leadership attracted a wide range of young men, many of whom received little positive recognition in school. By the time students reached seventh grade, when we started working with them, they had already witnessed and experienced a great deal of violence. When we started our program with a Saturday kickoff, students showed up laughing about a recent event where a sixth grader at school had been attacked by older students on the way home from school. Our leader, Alejandro Baldwin, cut them off. "That is nothing to laugh at," he told them, and they stopped.

On their own, with no one to show off for, and no one to feel threatened by, young men respond well to mentoring. EMU Young Men's Leadership Program did Saturday group mentoring for young men between seventh and twelfth grades, with a program that focused on responsibility, community service, and leadership development. By the end of the program, the twelfth graders were working with elementary and middle school boys on the same lessons they had learned earlier in the program. Group mentoring also helped the young men build small groups to support each other, which they needed at school and in their neighborhoods, when adult mentors were not around.

No one should pretend that working with 10–20 young men is an easy job. We had a team of four or five mentors working with that size group, and some Saturdays we left discouraged and exhausted. Arguing with young men about their use of bad language, disagreements about service projects, and just plain stubbornness can take its toll. On the other hand, events where we took young men, dressed in their best, to a restaurant to learn the etiquette of a business lunch, rank among the best days of our lives.

For any program for young men, physical activity is a prerequisite to real discussion. For our Saturday program for young men, we stocked our vans with basketballs, and found any court we could to burn off energy. The shift to less recess and fewer breaks in schools has given us a generation of fidgety young men, and giving them an outlet gives them a chance to be more centered. Once tired out a little, they can be more reflective, and open up about what is going on in their heads and in their lives.

Mentoring young men is a long-term process with many ups and downs. Mentoring is not a vaccine that prevents all problems and turns youth lives around. The book by three doctors, *The Pact*, illustrates this well (Davis, Jenkins, & Hunt, 2003). The young men in the book form an agreement to support one another in their journey from bleak Newark neighborhoods to medical (and dental) school. But their journey is rocky, and they get into many scrapes, even into college, that mentors need to help them dig out of. Young men in a mentoring program will need champions, people who can advocate on their behalf with parents, teachers, community members, and with the police and court system. Young men will be a test of mentors' commitment; the key is to pass the test.

CONVERSATION STARTERS

Young men are a tough crowd to connect with. Because they are much less talkative than their female peers and not inclined to be open about problems, maintaining a good conversation with young men is a challenge.

Pierre Rice suggests starting with talking about school. "How are your grades?" is a key question, as academic achievement can really limit what young men can do after high school. Other questions focus on whether young men are taking care of themselves or if others are taking care of them. "Where are you living right now?" and "Are you getting enough to eat?" are other good questions. Once young men know you care about them and their circumstances, they are more likely to open up about what is going on in their lives.

In his programming, Alejandro Baldwin takes on the big questions with young men, working to get them to allow themselves to be more transparent and vulnerable. "Who are you, and who do you want to be?" are two of his key questions for young men. He digs deeper, asking young men: "What parts of you do you like? What do you not like about yourself?" Finally, Alejandro works on what young men think their purpose in life is: "What are you called to do here?" These are tough questions, and take time and gradual gaining of trust to build up to, but they are key questions for young men to think about. (Adult men struggle with these questions, too.)

Young Men and Sports: A Big Bet

When young men map out their dream of college, they often put sports at the center. Unlike young women, they will structure their time by the sports season, not the calendar or academic year. There is nothing intrinsically wrong with this, as sports can help young people develop athletically, as well as learn service and leadership skills. But when sports becomes the "all in" bet for a young man, it means that other areas of life, such as academics, community involvement, and family, are de-emphasized.

This was not always true. A century ago, coaching and mentoring were synonymous. Before college sports became a multi-billion-dollar business, the coach of a college sports team "mentored" the students on his team. This included sports instruction and guidance, but also meant that a coach was invested in the leadership development, character education, and personal development of the young people he or she was responsible for. In an age when most students would never go on to pro athletics, coaching was more about getting people to develop skills to be successful in their future career, often business or a profession. With greater pressure to win, the coach is not always a mentor, and while athletics can provide great opportunities for mentoring, mentors need to think hard about the role of sports in the lives of their mentees.

The movie *Hoop Dreams* (James, 1994) opens with the powerful image of the scout, on the lookout for basketball talent in some of the roughest sections of Chicago. Throughout *Hoop Dreams*, the two young men featured in the movie focus heart and soul on basketball, with almost no attention to academics except as a road to pro sports. The entire system—coaches, recruiters, school officials—looks to these young men to win games, and no one is looking out for their long-term educational or personal interests. This situation, where sports and the rest of life collide, is when young people need a mentor most, someone who has no vested interest in their athletic career.

At the time of transition from middle school to high school, this investment in sports is pivotal in their academic lives. Middle school sports are a relatively small portion of students' lives. With limited choices and opportunities, students can pursue a middle school sport while also pursuing other after-school or academic activities. However, the summer before ninth grade, football camp begins for freshman football, and the investment becomes much more intense. This time of maximum investment, however, comes at a time when students face real academic hurdles.

It is at this critical moment that the power of football takes hold, as ninth-grade students struggle to remain eligible for their teams and to become part of a demanding fall sport. The drives to achieve in football, unlike school, are palpable. Social respect in high school is accorded to athletes, particularly in the top sports of football and basketball. Within the family, such male figures as fathers, uncles, and cousins can drive the need for respect through football achievement.

While these drives are seen across social groups, they affect students from low-income backgrounds more. Middle-class and higher families are aware of National Collegiate Athletics Association (NCAA) requirements and may push their children to maintain academic achievement that will, in fact, give them wider access to future educational and athletic opportunities. But without intensive planning and commitment on the part of the school, low-income students invest only in the game, and without the academic achievement to remain eligible in high school or eligible for college, they are making a highly leveraged investment, betting what they do not have on a dream.

What Mentors Can Do to Help with Sports

Like the young men in *Hoop Dreams*, most student-athletes in high school need someone to listen to and to ask them questions about what they want. High school students desperately need accurate information on their chances of pursuing a sports career, about what the role of college student-athlete requires, and what life is like as a pro athlete and after.

Just informing students about NCAA requirements for eligibility is a big first step, as these are often more stringent than high school standards. The NCAA has updated its requirements to a 2.3 GPA over a series of 16 core academic classes during high school. If students plan to have a shot at athletic scholarships at Division I schools, their high school academic record needs to be good enough to get them onto the field; low grades or SAT/ACT scores will mean they are not able to compete at top schools, or can be sent to the bench until their college grades prove that they are able to handle school and sports.

When it comes to issues of sports and achievement, students want to hear from athletes, not from their teachers, parents, or mentors. We have held programs to help high school students understand the world of college and professional athletics, and the impact of these events is powerful. One member of a panel, a former pro athlete who returned to college to graduate after his quick pro career, told aspiring high school student-athletes that NFL stands for "not for long," and that most pro players do not last five years. "I came back for my education," he told students and their parents, "because a degree lasts forever."

 TIE TO LEADERSHIP

How many young men are active in your program? How are young men treated in your building or program? How many top performers are males? How many low-performers/dropouts are males?

Being a consistent, supportive leader, mentor, and role model to young men can make a difference, particularly given the number of adults who have not fulfilled those promises. Addressing the issues of young men, particularly those that are most disruptive, and making those young men into leaders, can dramatically influence your program's impact and improve its culture.

 REFLECTION

— What images do you have of young men, particularly young men of color?
— How many of these images come from movies or other media? How many are negative? Positive? How do they shape your interactions with real-life young men?

Sample Daily Schedule for a Young Men's Leadership Day Program

Opening: as kids arrive, some physical activity, such as basketball, to help settle the young men.

Check-in for participants: how was the previous week for all youth and adults?

Opening discussion of key issue: outline of the day, discussion of "responsibility" with college professor.

Connection to real world: visit to workplace, such as hospital.

Lunch: during lunch, time for youth and adults to connect and continue discussion.

After lunch: service project, such as helping with local community garden.

Resources

Canada, G. (1995). *Fist, stick, knife, gun: A personal history of violence in America*. Boston, MA: Beacon Press.

Canada, G. (1998). *Reaching up for manhood: Transforming the lives of boys in America*. Boston, MA: Beacon Press.

Davis, S., Jenkins, G., & Hunt, R. (2003). *The pact: Three young men make a promise and fulfill a dream.* New York: Riverhead.

James, S. (1994). *Hoop Dreams.* United States: Home Vision Entertainment.

National Collegiate Athletics Association. *Don't get stuck on the bench in college.* http://blog.ncaa.org/GetTheGrades/#home

Rich, J. A. (2009). *Wrong place, wrong time: Trauma and violence in the lives of young black men.* Baltimore: Johns Hopkins University Press.

"You Gotta Push"

Mentoring Young Women to Success

Crisis for Young Women—Academic and Personal

Young women, and their place in schools, has changed. Decades ago, young women were steered away from academics in high school, with the expectation that they would only pursue higher education for their personal enrichment, or to make friends and find a husband. Today, looking at high school graduation ceremonies at urban schools, the top students are young women, and the majority of students walking to graduate are women. This is not just talk. Young women are the majority of students in higher education, pursuing a range of liberal arts and professional programs, particularly in education and health care. At the university I teach at, over 60 percent of incoming students are young women, and the same is true at many of the public universities and community colleges nation-wide.

Two economists who studied young women's academic achievement called their report *Leaving boys behind*, as young women were earning more and more As in high school, while many young men were dropping into the C range (Fortin & Oreopoulos, 2013). The study also found that young women, even those from low-income families, were raising their college and career aspirations, while young men were getting into more trouble at school, instead aiming towards a future in the military or the workplace directly after high school.

 **REFLECTION**

— The role of women in society was much different for most school leaders when they were growing up. Even when I was in school, I saw that quiet girls in my class were rewarded, while those who talked risked disapproval.

— What messages did families, schools, and society give women when you were in middle and high school?

— Have these messages remained the same? Are there different messages you want to express to young women now in your building or program? How will you get this message across?

While young women are achieving in remarkable ways, researchers still can point to ways in which they fall behind their male peers during adolescence, or become disconnected from such areas of study as math and science. Psychologist Carol Gilligan pointed out in her book, *In a different voice* (1993), that girls have different ways of talking and thinking as adolescents, focusing more on personal connections than abstract ideas of right and wrong. Mary Pipher's *Reviving Ophelia* (1994) focused on how girls lose their confidence, voice, and focus between late elementary and high school, fading into the woodwork in the classroom. Peggy Orenstein's book, *Schoolgirls (1994),* took this argument one step further, pointing out the ways that schools and teachers pushed girls aside through belittling them, discriminating against them, and failing to address harassment by peers.

The research is clear: girls can lose themselves in the middle and high school years. They lose self-confidence and develop a negative body image. As a result, their academic achievement can suffer. The writings of Gilligan, Pipher and Orenstein set off a revolution among parents and in schools. It would not be an exaggeration to say that a generation of mothers (and some fathers) took up the challenge of creating programs for young women to build and maintain voice, and to focus young women on academic achievement and careers in math and science fields. New programs focused on young women sought to bring together college-age women with teenagers to help young women keep their voice, raise their ambitions, and avoid the hazards of being an adolescent girl in America.

However, the research described earlier draws on a fairly limited set of experiences. Pipher's work focused on middle-class, white families, and

Orenstein's centers on (mostly) white, middle-class schools. As psychologists have studied wider populations of girls, particularly low-income and minority women, the portrait of teenage girls has broadened, revealing both some tremendous strengths of young women as well as some terrifying threats to their well-being.

The problems of young women in a low-income middle or high school are more immediate and frightening than "loss of voice." Girls in these settings are at risk from physical and sexual harassment and violence far beyond that experienced in middle-class schools. However, the literature on teenage girls misses the strengths these girls and families bring, and the extent to which these girls are passing their male counterparts on the road to college.

Strengths of Young Women

When student teachers from middle-class backgrounds start teaching in low-income schools, the first thing they notice is that the girls are tough, and if they look closer, they notice that the girls are strong. Unlike the image of Ophelia—the swooning, listless Dane who haunts the literature of adolescent girls—the girls in the schools we work in are ambitious, loud, opinionated, smart, funny, hard-working, and sometimes seem out of control. Their verbal arguments with peers are loud and spirited, and when roused, their fights can explode into massive group confrontations with more than a dozen girls participating.

High school girls in low-income schools, particularly African-American girls, show little of the drop off in self-esteem that is seen in the broader culture. These girls show a level of self-acceptance that is uncommon in a mainstream culture that defines only the thinnest girls "pretty." Insulated and protected by a vibrant African-American culture, strong female role models, and groups of friends with similar views, girls in lower-income schools can envision an academic and career future for themselves in a way that few of their male counterparts can.

Academically, girls in low-income schools rule the school. Girls overall outperform boys in high school by 0.23 grade points, i.e., by about a quarter of a letter grade (Corbett & Hill, 2008, p. 52). They complete high school at a higher rate, then earn more bachelor's degrees each year. Among African-American students, these statistics are even starker. Women hold roughly twice as many bachelor's degrees as men in the African-American community, and earn roughly twice as many degrees per year (90,000 to 40,000). African-

American women form a larger proportion of college degree holders than African-American men, Hispanic men and women, or Asian-Pacific men or women.

In one of our local schools, young African-American women have the highest graduation rate in the school, above the level of white men and white women. Young women are at the top of their classes, and they express high aspirations for college and for their careers. In math and science achievement, these girls score above their peers, and their grades and test scores are in strong contrast to the idea that girls lose interest in math, science, or academics in order to pursue boys. Looking at our achievement of students in eighth grade, girls outnumber boys with As in both advanced and basic math classes. At the bottom of the class, fewer girls fail math than boys, with close to a 2:1 advantage for girls.

Challenges for Young Women

While girls may outperform boys academically in low-income schools, they do so within an unstable and often violent context. Girls may work somewhat harder in school, may earn higher GPAs, and may be on track for college, but the physical and sexual violence that is part of their environment can destroy them at any time. Girls' achievement in high school might be best understood as a performance on a wire, where the young women may be rising above the pack, but the danger of falling is ever present.

Girls in this urban context still face challenges far beyond those of their higher-income peers. Violence, and violence against women, is a fact of life in the neighborhoods and schools in which young women live each day. Many girls face violence in school, with a sizable minority (19 percent) reporting that they had a physical fight last year. This can take the form of harassment and stalking, or escalate into assault or rape. Girls report being bullied at a rate far higher than boys (18 percent vs. 21 percent) in person, as well as online (10 percent vs. 24 percent). More serious crimes, such as kidnapping and murder, are not remote possibilities in these areas, but the result of being at the wrong place in the wrong time (Youth Risk Behavior Survey, 2013).

In Jody Miller's (2008) study of young women in St. Louis, she points out that girls from inner-city neighborhoods witness and experience a level of violence that is far higher than in suburban areas. Of teenage girls in her study, nearly all (94 percent) had seen someone hit, a majority (77 percent) had witnessed gun violence, nearly half (46 percent) had witnessed a robbery, and over a third (34 per cent) reported that they were present when someone was being killed. School was a place where girls were targeted. A majority reported that they had been called hurtful names by boys and been the targets of unwanted sexual comments. Almost half (49 percent) reported being grabbed or touched in ways that made them feel uncomfortable. This verbal violence could escalate into sexual violence, as sizable proportions of girls reported being pressured to have unwanted sex (37 percent), sexual assault or molestation (26 percent), and attempts at sexual violence against them (17 percent).

Sexuality and risk taking can also be a challenge. Like teenage boys, whose high self-esteem and belief in immortality is associated with risk taking, girls can face a similar set of challenges. According to the 2013 Youth Risk Behavior Survey, almost one in four young women in high school report having had sex at least once, and about one in three report being sexually active at the time surveyed. While sexual risk taking is a characteristic shared by young men and women, it is women for whom the consequence of pregnancy is possible, slowing down and making more difficult (but not necessarily stopping) educational or career progress. Many of the girls in our program professed a desire to go to college, but once they graduated from high school and no longer had ready access to mentors, they became pregnant and stopped out of college. Though they may return to their education, many are travelling in the same path that their mothers did, a profoundly discouraging pattern.

Teenage girls' strengths can also be their weakness. Researchers have found that girls think more about relationships, but this can become a weakness when those relationships sour. A single incident of "mean eye" and its consequences has sucked up a day of staff time at one of our sites, as the two students and their friends postured and jostled over perceived disrespect for hours.

The Internet, social media, and cell phones have done a great deal to enable this risk taking. The ability to take pictures or video of one's self or friends is fraught with peril, as images of girls can circulate widely with almost instant speed. Students can also use a range of digital apps to contact others they do not know to set up a rendezvous, an event that surprised us on a college tour field trip out of state. One of our students used Facebook to contact young men in another city to come and meet her at the hotel we had booked for a field trip, leading to a confrontation in the parking lot between the men responding to the post and the chaperones. Access to social media opens young women to contact with predators, usually older men looking for prospects.

The cell phone or smart phone, regarded by many parents as a safety device, can often be the opposite. Calls and texting can suck participants from where they are and what they are doing, into a digital social world that burns their time and exhausts them with social conflicts. We have had to send students home from our residential Upward Bound program on our campus for late-night Facebook drama, with the youth unable to give up their digital soap opera, even when it meant losing out on educational opportunity. Phones and the Internet are used extensively for taunting and psychological torture, and our program has banned their use on our field trips as a result.

Building Young Women's Leadership Programs

The problems young women face have produced a nation-wide response. Church groups, mentoring programs, and grants were set up to nurture young women from this loss of voice, and to increase their academic achievement, particularly in math and science. Many programs were founded to create "hardiness zones" for young women, where they could be protected from the forces, inside and outside school, which were undermining their ambitions.

For young women in low-income schools, these needs are both the same and different. Two models that have taken root are Femtoring programs, which bring college students to low-income middle schools for group-mentoring activities, and leadership groups, which use two adult mentors to work with a group of female students around their own issues. Both of these models draw in powerful ways on the strengths of these communities.

The group-mentoring model, as seen elsewhere in this book, offers young women a range of possible role models and mentors, and allows that relationship to build over time. Allowing girls to have a voice in the topics they want to address allows adults to serve as guides, rather than teachers, able to connect girls to important resources and opportunities. The issues that these groups tackle include body image, competition among girls, building supportive friendships, dating violence, and avoiding risky behaviors. Showing young women the range of opportunities available to them, such as local colleges or workplaces, can have a powerful impact, as can local service projects that help take the focus off present issues and problems.

In successful mentoring programs for young women, building leadership and doing community service are powerful tools to help participants achieve. This means helping give young women a sense that they can be leaders, that they can make a difference, and that their voice matters. While sitting and talking about issues can be a valuable activity, young women also need opportunities to get out into their schools or their communities and make a difference through service. Since many of the issues facing young women are based on how they are perceived, taking the spotlight off them, and having experiences that bring perspective to their issues, can be helpful.

Sample activities for young women's groups or individual mentoring

- Career activities or inventory
- Media portrayals of young women
- Competitiveness among young women
- College visits—nearby or out of state
- Volunteering
- Backpacking trip/hiking
- Lunch or dinner where students learn etiquette

When we asked participants in our Young Women's Leadership Program which programs had meant the most to them, they pointed out to activities that got them out of their immediate surroundings. Girls are "stuck in one place," one young woman said, and trips, particularly the out-of-state college trip, made a big difference for her. The girls reported that visiting Spelman College, a historically black college for women, gave a new perspective on what college could be like.

Young women's programs draw from powerful traditions. Young women have always had a stronger urge to get together and talk than men, and young women's leadership groups tap into this desire to share experiences. The adult women who run our girls' leadership groups are able to tap into a wide variety of resources—sororities, young women's social groups, service organizations—that can pull together programming and funding with a few phone calls or emails. Our most powerful programming for young women brought together girls and adult female relatives (mothers, aunts) for a dinner at a local community college. A facilitator worked with the group to talk about what the adult women had wished they had done differently in life, and what hopes they had for the young women.

Leaders for these groups need to be carefully selected. One of our young women told us that the leader of the mentoring group makes all the difference: "If I don't like them, ain't no reason to be coming." Teenage girls have an amazingly sensitive ear for adults talking down to them or scolding them, and a single tone of voice or look can affect their attitude about a program. But the right individuals, if they can demonstrate that they genuinely care for the young women, can make a world of difference.

The community tradition of aunts, family friends, teachers, and counselors serving as a support, or surrogate mother, also strengthens programming. It is not unusual in the communities in which we work for young women to bring their problems or issues to trusted adult women in the community, especially when conflict with parents is at the center of the issue. Programs and schools that are able to tap into these traditions, and use them to their benefit, can have tremendous results. I believe the higher-than-average graduation rate for young women is attributable to this wide and deep support network for young women, while young men often try to go it alone.

 REAL PEOPLE

Jaclyn Stevens

Setting up mentoring programs for young women is a challenge. Teams of mentors work best, with at least one from the local neighborhood. Women from many different backgrounds can work effectively as mentors for young women, as long as they are able to express caring and concern in the right way. Jaclyn Stevens worked with our Ladies of Leadership program at Wayne High School, and found that it was a struggle to just get the students to focus on what was important to them. She noted: "It was a struggle to help girls keep their priorities straight, and to make decisions consistently."

The girls struggled to show up for the program, even though they were involved in few other activities. A few had jobs, but the program also had to compete against peers, social life, and boyfriends. The girls' family lives were chaotic, with no clear adult to contact when problems arose. The program focused on getting girls out of the high school—walking to another nearby school to do community service, walking to a local health center for a tour, visits to local colleges—anything to get girls out of their immediate surroundings. These helped the girls have more ideas about what to do when they left high school. Jaclyn remembers asking the girls: "Just where do you want to go? It was fun when their guard was let down and they told me what they wanted to be and what they were passionate about. When they could let me know what they were really thinking, it was really cool."

 ## TIE TO LEADERSHIP

The issues that young women face can be hot-button issues. How comfortable are you talking to young people about the way they dress? About their online image? About their family and friends?

Work with young women can stretch leaders and mentors out of their comfort zone. Being able to express your questions and concerns clearly and appropriately is an important professional skill to develop and hone. If you feel uncomfortable with these discussions, seek out leaders and mentors who are strong in this area and pair up for these discussions.

 ## CONVERSATION STARTERS

— For young women, the connections they have to others (parents, peers) can overwhelm the more abstract issues of college, career, or academic achievement. These questions can sometimes help clarify issues for young women:

— Who is supporting you in pursuing your goals? Your family? Your friends? Your teachers?

— What do you want for yourself in the future? Who can help support you? Are there mentors we need to find for you to get you to where you want to be?

Resources

Corbett, C., & Hill, C. (2008). *Where the girls are: The facts about gender equity in education.* Distributed by ERIC Clearing House.

Fortin, N. M., & Oreopoulos, P. (2013). *Leaving boys behind: Gender disparities in high academic achievement.* Cambridge, MA: National Bureau of Economic Research.

Gilligan, C. (1993). *In a different voice: Psychological theory and women's development.* Cambridge, MA: Harvard University Press.

Miller, J. (2008). *Getting played: African-American girls, urban inequality, and gendered violence.* New York: New York University Press.

Orenstein, P. (1994). *Schoolgirls: Young women, self-esteem, and the confidence gap.* New York: Doubleday.

Pipher, M. B. (1994). *Reviving Ophelia: Saving the selves of adolescent girls.* New York: Putnam.

Data from the Youth Risk Behavior Surveillance System is available at www.cdc.gov/healthyyouth/data/yrbs/index.htm

Becoming a Mentor

Setting and Keeping High Expectations

Warning: Do Not Trip Over the Low Expectations

One of the hardest things for me to accept in running programs for young people is how often adults in schools and other institutions have profoundly low expectations of the students they serve. As someone who works to train teachers when they are in college, I was shocked to find out that teachers had far lower expectations and hope for students than they themselves did or their parents. In the first year of our GEAR UP program, when the students were in grade 7, over 90 percent of the students we worked with expected to go to college, and over 80 percent of their parents expected the same. However, the proportion of their teachers was closer to 40 percent. By twelfth grade, with a lot of work from our staff and a great deal of effort by the building leaders, over 70 percent of teachers saw college potential in their students.

 TIE TO LEADERSHIP

Researchers have shown that teachers' and adults' expectations of students become a self-fulfilling prophecy, back to the Pygmalion effect that I read about when I was training to be a teacher. While educational scholars and teachers have been debating how "real" this effect is since the sixties, when the experiment was conducted by Rosenthal and Jacobson (1968), the findings remain important. When teachers believe that they are teaching capable, smart students, they do a much better job. When faced with students who they believe are unmotivated or untalented, they do a much worse job.

The steps to making sure your program is setting high expectations for participants and maintaining them over time are:

1. **Clarifying** what you expect from mentors and mentees
2. **Building** high expectations into the program
3. **Sustaining** those expectations over time
4. **Celebrating** when mentors and mentees meet their goals.

What Goals Does Your Mentoring Program Have?

The first step to building high expectations is to clarify the one or two areas in which you or your program plan to make a difference. This might be as broad as academic achievement, or as narrow as a young person avoiding further contact with juvenile court. These goals should be expressed in a sentence or so, and they should be understandable by both your mentors and the students you are working with.

The second part of clarifying is to understand the range of what you can realistically achieve. There may be a goal of every single student in the program eventually attending college, but for many youth, this goal might be out of reach at first. To be honest with mentors and with those who support your program, such as funders, it is important to set measurable, realistic, attainable goals for your program. This does not mean your goals should not be ambitious, but that you should take into account where you are starting from (your baseline) before setting a target for your achievement.

Building high expectations is important for everyone involved in mentoring. Both students and adults can get caught in the low expectations they can be surrounded with. Field trips to other programs or schools that serve similar students but are high achieving can be the key to building higher expectations in your program. Seeing, hearing, and being in a successful program is irreplaceable, as mentors can read about successful programs and easily think "theirs are not our students."

Next, mentors and mentees should be clear on what the goal of their relationship is and how to get there. Programs that are not based on the goals of the mentees, however well-funded and well-intentioned, almost always fail to reach their full potential. The mentee must have a voice in setting the goals, and the mentor must be able to work with those goals. The opening sessions of any mentoring relationship or program should give both mentor and mentee a clear vision of what success means for their relationship, and one or two clear goals to pursue.

Sustaining expectations is the hardest part of keeping a mentoring program going. This is when mentors have to keep their mentee's eyes "on the prize" and making progress towards their goals. This may mean that the program needs to keep in touch with mentors to keep the effort moving, or in some cases, it might need to rethink pairings or groupings that seem to have settled into an unproductive groove. Highlighting mentees who are really making strides can help set a positive example for mentors and mentees alike.

It may be necessary to bring mentors and mentees back together from time to time, to remind them of the purpose of the program and the goals that everyone involved in the program shares. As your program grows, having graduates of the program able to return and talk about its goals will be another tool available to help keep expectations and energy high.

Finally, working with youth is hard, and requires a lot of patience. Celebrations of program or mentee success are important, and bringing together mentors to share experiences, and feel valued for their work, is vital. These events do not need to be lavish, but are vital for programmatic renewal. As mentors and mentees see participants moving on to greater success, this will keep their expectations high for their own mentoring relationship and for their own future.

 **REFLECTION**

How are you celebrating success in your program? How are you getting out stories of success to your supporters? Many programs just try to do difficult work every day without taking time to savor small victories, or to tell the community about the impact that they made. This does not help build sustainable programs or build community support for your work.

What to Do When a Mentor or Mentee Does Not Share Your Expectations

While people who get involved in mentoring, as a mentor or mentee, almost always do so for positive reasons, there are times when people just do not buy into the program enough to be effective. Adults may sign up to mentor in order to have a social outlet, meet other interesting mentors, or relive their youth. They may be unable to do the hard work of helping youth set goals and then holding them accountable. In this case, it makes sense to move the adult from that role as soon as possible, but often it can mean finding a different role within the program.

This does not always mean dismissing people from mentoring programs. We have had adults who were not effective as individual mentors, but when it came to talking to groups of young people about their careers and professions, they were excellent. Look for the right niche for adults or young people who are not ready for the full commitment just yet, as they may have much to contribute, and they may grow towards that fuller role in the future.

👥 REAL PEOPLE

Melissa Calabrese has worked in 21st Century Community Learning Center programs and GEAR UP programs all of her professional life. She currently works at John Glenn High School in Wayne, Michigan, running an after-school program that focuses on building youth voice among students who do not always feel listened to in their school or their family. She has taken this mission global with TedEd, in which she has worked with students to create Ted talks about educational issues. These are professionally staged, digitally recorded, and submitted to Ted. Each year, at least a few have been featured on the TedEd channel, giving the young people a global platform for their ideas.

Resource

Rosenthal, R. & Jacobson, L. (1968). *Pygmalion in the classroom: Teacher expectation and pupils' intellectual development.* New York: Holt, Rinehart and Winston.

9 Asking Questions to Clarify Goals

Asking Questions to Help Mentees Think

In our own lives, we have worked for and with people who were better or worse listeners. For many of us, when we were growing up and going through school, authority figures were almost always directive. They listened up until the point where they knew what you should do, and then they told you. End of conversation. On the other end of the spectrum are listeners so indirect that we are never sure what they are telling us at all. They speak in riddles or clichés, without revealing their thoughts or feelings.

 **REFLECTION**

— Think back to a time you were just not listened to at school and a situation where you felt truly listened to.
— What emotions did these situations provoke in you at the time?
— What lessons do you draw from the experiences?

In education, we all try to be somewhere in between these two points, in what many writers have called the "coaching zone," where the person listening tries to hear out the person, paraphrase for understanding, then offer some key questions to help the person solve their own problems, thus building capacity and confidence. This is a tall order to fill, even for experienced leaders and mentors.

Choosing words so carefully can be difficult for people used to a casual flow of conversation. But we should try to learn from this new literature on cognitive coaching, so that the discussions we have with young people are meaningful and real. They also can help the individual make better decisions on his or her own, not just when a mentor is around to talk to.

This cognitive coaching model includes:

1. Really listening to someone, with your whole body and your whole mind. This requires putting away the phone, closing the laptop screen, and tuning out all the other noise in your head. This kind of active listening takes practice.

2. Asking questions first to get some clarity about what the other person is feeling or thinking. These are not judgmental questions—"What were you thinking, young man?"—but honest questions designed to get more information.

3. Asking questions that assume the good intentions of the other person, and that seek to help him or her clarify what the next steps should be. These questions should be positive in tone, and should imply that the other person has given real thought to the situation in advance of the conversations.

4. Summarizing the next steps and asking how you can be of help to support the young person. This means that the young person is in charge of the situation, and the mentor is there to support and guide.

Another similar approach to working with young people is "motivational interviewing," which comes out of work in clinical psychology to help clients make changes in their own lives and stick to them. In motivational interviewing, questions are used to help the mentee understand his or her own strengths, to clarify goals, to understand the discrepancy between their goals and behaviors, and to make a plan to change. Through empathetic listening, accurate summarizing, and helping the mentee create a plan for change, motivational interviewing can help encourage people to make changes that they want to make, but often have trouble following through on or sustaining.

Questions to Get Started

Every conversation needs to start, and questions are a good way to get a relationship underway. Some opening questions I have found valuable include the following.

What is your goal?

In Japan, people routinely use a *daruma* to set a goal, filling in one of the blank eyes to indicate that they have a goal in mind. This means that once the goal is set, the task is already half completed.

What do you want to see happen in the next year
(or semester/month)?

Letting students know that they have a future, and that the future can be different from the past, can have a positive impact.

What do you want to avoid? What are you scared of?

Likewise, young people can also gain motivation from looking at the possibility of failure. While this can overwhelm their thinking at times, and while they are often better at pointing out other people's failures than seeing their own, this can be a productive question.

Who are people you know now that you want to be like?

Helping young people see that there are people around them who are positive and doing positive things is important. While they may not want to follow the career path of someone they know, they can at least see aspects of them that remind them of what they want to be.

Going Deeper: Ways to Follow Up

It is not enough to have good opening questions in mentoring. While I have often been asked to set up "speed mentoring" programs to pair young people with adults for a few minutes, good mentoring requires strategies to go deeper. In this way, mentoring is like a game of chess. Good openings can start the game on the right foot, but follow-up questions are the middle game, where more pieces can come into play.

What led you to this goal? Talk me through your thinking.

It does not pay to contradict young people about their goals and dreams, but questions about why they think what they do can be helpful for them to clarify

their ideas and plans. The goal here is not to belittle or contradict the young person's ideas, but to grasp them better.

What is a first step you can take towards this goal right now?

Students are often lost about where to start. You can help them identify one concrete step they can take towards a goal. This can be a step you do with them, like looking at a website for a college together. It also can be something that the student needs to do on his or her own, such as starting a college essay.

Who can support you in pursuit of this goal right now?

Students need a team to help them achieve what they want. As a mentor, you are part of the team, but there are other key members who need to be part of the process.

Can I help you draw up a plan or make a list?

Adults should not swoop in and save their mentees from their own dis-organization. But asking permission to help out with organizing a task can help model how adults organize their endeavors. I almost always suggest the young person is holding the paper and making the list, not the adult.

What do you think will be the most challenging thing about pursuing this goal?

If young people can think ahead and visualize what might be difficult, they can be better prepared.

What was a situation like the one you are talking about now? How did you handle that?

If young people have a feeling that they have already overcome similar obstacles, they are more likely to persist in their efforts.

Where do you prefer to spend time—home or school?

This opens up a discussion both in terms of how things are going at school, but also whether the student's relationships at home are OK, too. How a student answers this can lead to questions about teachers, parents, siblings—many different directions, depending on where the student is experiencing more success.

Last-Ditch Attempts: Questions to Ask When You Are at the End of Your Rope

At the end of the day, not every mentee is going to see a way forward that is safe, legal, and productive. There are going to be times when young people are caught in a spiral of negativity, and are not able to see a positive way out. At moments when things seem lost, it pays to ask some final questions.

Do you see a purpose for yourself in life? Do you think there is a plan for you for the future?

This can sound a little religious or spiritual, and that is intentional. Ultimately, if young people do not see a future for themselves that is at least somewhat hopeful, then they will engage in the riskiest behaviors possible, confident that they will not survive to see the consequences of their actions. This is a profound illusion that young people have, because the consequences of young people's poorly thought out actions resonate in the lives of those around them, particularly in the lives of the people who love them.

If young people can see that there may be a future for them, even a chance of a time when things would be better, there is something to keep them off the wrong road. However, if they really do not see any future but pain, there is nothing more that a mentor can do. A professional counselor would have more adequate tools for the job.

 TIE TO LEADERSHIP

Frameworks for Goals

Most of us who have taken coursework in leadership have been taught a few frameworks to set effective goals. The traditional method is SMART goals—Specific, Measurable, Achievable, Realistic, Timely. This can be as simple as setting a goal of filling out five college applications by a specific date.

Another research-based method of setting goals is WOOP—Wish, Outcome, Obstacle, Plan. This involves defining the goal (wish), how it might make you feel if accomplished (outcome), what are some obstacles you can predict (external or internal), and how you can mitigate the obstacle (plan). There is a WOOP framework for applying to college available online, as well as a WOOP app for the iPhone or Android. WOOP helps young people connect to positive feelings of achievement ("I'll feel smart and relieved if I complete the five college applications"), and is also explicit about the blocks that students may face ("My parents may not support me in this").

Resources

www.woopmylife.org/ This includes information and links to the WOOP app.

http://roadtripnation.com/roadmap A resource for exploring careers, featuring video from a wide range of folks in areas that interest students.

http://careervillage.org A place where students can ask questions about their career ideas and get ideas about from real-world professionals.

10 | Connecting to Parents and Guardians

Myths About Low-Income Parents

Parents get blamed.

When students come to school in low-income areas, many teachers, and even mentors, assume that there is low parental support for college going. Mentors can feel like they are doing the parents' job when they are helping students apply to college, and they can get resentful.

Scholars are often worse, blaming parents for multiple problems in education. In their 2003 book *No excuses: Closing the racial gap in learning*, Abigail and Stephan Thernstrom argue that poor parental support and low expectations are major reasons behind the racial achievement gap in American schools.

While many families struggle with academic success for their children, those of us who work with college access and mentoring programs see no shortage of parental support and ambition for the students in the program. What is often lacking is the knowledge of how to translate hopes into specific goals.

Surveys of parents and focus groups indicate that parents in working-class and lower-income areas are far more supportive of college and higher education than researchers and policy makers give them credit for. They are actually as ambitious for their children as middle-class parents. The vast majority of parents (92 percent) in our GEAR UP project expect their children to go to college, with African-American parents scoring slightly higher than white parents on this measure. Running a mentoring program, you do not need to convince parents that college is a good thing. You do have to show them how to get there.

While parents support higher education for their children, they also recognize that they face difficult hurdles on the way to those goals. Working- and lower-class parents cite the complexities of family life, difficulty negotiating a changing educational terrain, and their own lack of success in reaching higher education as formidable barriers to their children's success. Parents look to schools and to other college access programs to fill these gaps and to make sure that students are able to attain their dreams of a college education.

The Changing, Complex, Unstable Family

During a focus group with parents in a working-class/low-income community in Michigan, a parent was interrupted by a cell phone call at the start of the session. He took the call, then told the assembled parents and researchers: "My wife and I are getting a divorce, selling our house. That was my daughter, someone's here to see the house, you have to be home. No, I don't have to be home. I'm sorry for that." This cell call is just one slice of the life of many of the parents programs work with. The end of a marriage, selling a house at a loss, needing to be in more than one place at a time—all of these events point to a situation where a child's goal of college might be derailed by circumstances beyond her or his control.

Single-parent status, divorce, remarriage, and other forms of family disruption have created more turbulent upbringings for many children in low-income schools. In many cases, it might not be clear at any one moment who is caring for a young person. As one of my staff members put it: "You did not know where to call home. It could change each week." This creates difficult circumstances for some students since, while the new family may provide greater financial resources than a single-family household, it brings a new instability to the situation as well. Academic problems exist in the context of a difficult and unstable family situation that makes it difficult to address only academics.

Grandparents raising grandchildren has also become a common theme in programs, as one grandparent told a focus group:

> My husband and I have a blended family, and we have seven children between us. I have five daughters. But the reason I am involved with GEAR UP is for grandchildren. I have guardianship of three—one is 12, the one that's in the program. And I also thank God for this program and all of you because being a grandparent . . . guardianship didn't start right away, that happened in February. His mother and step-father have addiction problems with drugs.

Programs need to expect that a wide range of caregivers will be in their "parent group," many of whom have wide-ranging and multiple family responsibilities.

All of the above family forms are more complex, less stable, and less able to help students attain their goals of a college education. Families in the midst of these kinds of severe disruptions, such as divorce, remarriage, changing households, or moving, are less able to foster their children's academic and social success. Both divorced and remarried households are less successful at having children attend college, and are both more likely to produce children who are poor as adults.

Changes in Education Leave Parents in the Dust

Parents also feel ill-prepared to help their children navigate the new curricula in math, reading, writing, and science that have been developed and implemented in the last two decades. Programs such as Everyday Math, Writing Workshops, and Inquiry-Based Science programs test the limits of parents' ability to help their children with homework and school decisions. The new "Common Core" has almost nothing in common with what many parents had in their own schooling, further leading to confusion. New ways to calculate arithmetic answers can leave parents feeling frustrated, and Next Generation Science standards that stress scientific thinking are the opposite of the memorization that most of us faced in our own high school science classes.

Many parents are motivated to help their children with schoolwork, but are overwhelmed by the time the child reaches middle school-level work. One mother told us about her daughter:

> She had been bringing home Es all the time; I was like, oh my goodness, what are we going to do? I can't help her because I went to school how many years ago? I'm lost. I'm like, "Sorry sweetie, I just can't do it. Ya know, I just can't give you that help."

Parents struggle to help with the logistics of homework, such as the journey of books and assignments to and from school, and to the teacher, but often feel helpless to address the content of the work as well.

Parents also point to changes in the curriculum that make it more difficult for them to help. Another parent told us that the curriculum is so new as to be a whole new world to anyone who went to middle and high school a generation ago in the district:

> When we went to school, it's totally different than what they're teaching now. Like sixth grade, I can remember this—those 100 multiplication things, you had to do them in five minutes. Time tests. We did those dittos. Now they're doing algebra and pre-algebra and all that stuff, I don't even know.

As children move into middle and high school, when stakes are higher and planning for college becomes more important, parents' ability to help drops dramatically.

Researcher Anne Lareau (2011) has pointed out that for many working-class and low-income parents, school is not a place that they have felt comfortable or find easy to navigate. Their own experience as students can cast a shadow over their interactions with school, and schools themselves do much to make parents feel that they are not doing enough for their children. Mentoring programs can help parents and students feel more empowered to take advantage of what a school offers, and can help them find opportunities for skills and talent development that are second nature in wealthier homes.

Navigating the path to college is also difficult for parents who did not attend one. One parent told us:

> I think that when we went to school and we graduated from high school, that was the main focus, was graduating. And unfortunately, I did not go on to college, and I would have loved to, but other things got in the way. Children got in the way, not in the way, but they were born, new life now. And my whole goal in high school was to graduate and to have children, and I did that.

For this generation, the dream of a high school diploma is faded, as the earning power it represents has eroded. Instead, parents face trying to help their children navigate new hurdles on the way to a college education.

For people a generation ago, the college application process was simpler. For many families, applying to a community college or a state university was a matter of filling out a few forms. Since public university tuition was so low, financial aid was not always an issue. Many students could work summers and during the school year to pay for school, room, and board. But with state support for education eroding, students can no longer make enough to put a dent in their bills. And the college application process that might have been two or three applications decades ago can now be an extensive campaign of ten or more college applications, many to out-of-state and private institutions.

Parents Need Help Seeking Help

Parents in working- and lower-class communities are also suspicious of their children receiving too much help, whether in terms of academics or mentoring. Unlike many middle- and upper-class families, where tutoring, extra help, and parental support for academic work is the norm, parents in working- and lower-class areas feel that school is the child's job. One parent told us:

> I am a little concerned that the GEAR UP program might be a little enabling because I love my daughter dearly, but she will not do for herself if someone will do for her. And so I'm a little concerned about that. Time will tell.

Parents who did not receive academic help in their own academic career have trouble negotiating the system, and even in understanding when help is required for their child.

Parents also ward off their children's requests for help on homework, both out of insecurity about knowing the material, and out of a sense that they have mastered middle and high school alone and their children need to do the same. This sense that students should be "rugged individuals" works against their academic success, and ultimately their college plans. Competing with middle-class students who can pay for academic tutoring and private admissions counseling, low-income families can end up without the help they need to level the playing field.

How Mentoring Programs Can Reach Parents

The first thing mentoring programs can do for parents and guardians is to respect their role, listen to their concerns, and meet them halfway. The vast majority of parents want only the best for their children, and discussions with them, even by phone, often help bridge the gap between parents/children and programs. Programs can also build chances for parents to participate, in college visits, in trips, even in a simple celebration to mark the end of the program. Parents need to feel comfortable with the opportunities that their children have, and this can take time.

Mentors and mentoring programs can also "catch kids doing something good." When parents realize a call is from school, they brace for the worst—suspension, detention, expulsion, failure. Schools often only call for negative reasons. Mentors and mentoring programs can contact parents to report some good news, improvement, a goal met, even just encouragement to come to a program. Even small tokens, such as awards for improving grades or attendance, may be the only positive recognition a student and his or her family have ever received from a school

Finally, parents and guardians need to have their own dreams and frustrations acknowledged. Many women restart stalled college careers while their daughters are in school, to show their children that anything is possible. Anything mentoring programs can do to show respect to the aspirations of both parents and young people will be repaid in loyalty and appreciation. As much as possible, programs should take a "two-generation" approach, helping both the parent and the children to do the best that they can.

Some programming has tried to tap into parents' experiences to help the students. One of our Bright Futures sites asked parents at a family event to write about a failure in their own life, in order to help parents and youth rethink the notion of "failure." The parents responded well to the opportunity, many opening up about serious setbacks and disappointments. This helped lead to a discussion of helping young people reframe failure as a chance to learn.

TIE TO LEADERSHIP

As school and teacher leaders, most of the feedback that you get from parents is negative, and from a relatively small number of parents. Pareto's 80/20 rule definitely applies to parent interaction: about 20 percent of parents will take up 80 percent of the available time. This squeezes out the ideas and viewpoints of many parents who lack the time or inclination to pester programs and leaders. Reaching out to parents to share good news about a student or to ask an opinion can put you in contact with the full spectrum of parents.

Research has shown that low-income parents, while they believe in their children's education and want to be involved, have fewer avenues than their wealthy peers to be involved in schools in the traditional ways, such as parent–teacher organizations and fundraising. If you want more parents involved in mentoring programs, it is important to ask them how they want to be involved, how much they can do, and when is the best time for them. Many parents are happy to take on tasks as long as they do not interfere with work or family responsibilities, and they often feel honored to be asked.

Researcher Joyce Epstein (2002) identifies six different ways for parents to be more involved at school, and all approaches apply to mentoring programs (in or out of school) as well.

1. Support parents in their role as parents through information and support.
2. Build effective communication between program and parents.
3. Provide opportunities for parents to volunteer in the program.
4. Provide information to help parents better help their children make decisions.
5. Involve parents in decision-making.
6. Help parents locate and navigate resources to help their children.

Think about ways your mentoring program or school could support Epstein's list of ways to engage parents.

Resources

Epstein, J. L. (2002). *School, family, and community partnerships: Your handbook for action.* 2nd ed. Thousand Oaks, CA: Corwin Press.

Lareau, A. (2011). *Unequal childhoods: Class, race and family life.* Berkeley, CA: University of California Press.

Thernstrom, A. M., & Thernstrom, S. (2003). *No excuses: Closing the racial gap in learning.* New York: Simon & Schuster.

Basics of Post-Secondary Success

Mapping Out a Plan with a Mentee

Young people have a lot of ideas about how the future will be. However, due to their lack of experience and the way that their brains develop, their maps do not always correspond to the shape of the terrain to come.

 **REFLECTION**

What did you want to do when you grew up when you were the same age as your mentee? I wanted to be a scientist, then a fighter pilot, then settled on public-interest lawyer. I switched to history in college, with no regrets. I use this story with young people to illustrate that you have to be open to changing ideas and majors based on what is really going to work for you.

Cognitive scientists have shown that teenagers have some real weaknesses when it comes to their views about the future. They struggle with long-term thinking and can get stuck in looking for short-term gratification and pleasure. This makes them very susceptible to distractions, particularly ones that are fun, dangerous, or forbidden. This works against developing grit, the tenacity that it takes to accomplish a task even when it is unpleasant, uncomfortable, or seems hopeless (Steinberg, 2014).

Teenagers are also susceptible, for better or worse, to peer pressure. Surrounded by poor role models, toxic peer groups, and "frenemies," teens can become self- and other-destructive more easily than adults. They feel almost physical pain from social rejection, and thus avoid it at all costs. On the plus side, when surrounded with positive peer groups, teens are even more likely to act responsibly and decently than their adult counterparts.

When it comes to making a plan, it will help to get students to try to think much more long term than they are used to, and it may help for them to imagine their peers with them on this journey. In addition, I have found that even when young people can come up with an ultimate goal at the end of their journey, the intermediate steps they need to take to get there are often absent.

Working with Young People on a Map

In order to get students to think about their future, I have found mapping invaluable. To do this, I provide large sheets of paper or poster board, along with coloring pencils, crayons, and markers. While this may seem a little low-tech, the larger paper helps encourage more expansive thinking, and the crayons and pencils tap into the hope for the future that people have when they are younger. I give students a beginning point (now) and an end point (college or career), and some key points to get on the map (high school graduation, etc.). I try to leave as much as possible for the young people to come up with, as their own ideas about the future always take a different focus than my own ideas.

Young Women's Maps

Young women tend to make more intricate and detailed maps than their male peers. This could be because they are a little more mature and because they may see a wider range of opportunities available in the world. Many colleges are over 60 percent female at this point, and this can affect college aspirations. For many young women, seeing their sisters, mothers, aunts, and cousins attend and conquer college can be an inspiring experience.

However, the sheer range of interests and talents that young women list out can make for a confusing map. Some of the areas women may want to pursue might involve little formal education (e.g., a career as a model), while others involve decades of training (e.g., a medical career). Some have pointed out that women's range of talents can work against them in pursuing careers in difficult fields, such as STEM (science, technology, engineering, and mathematics), or pursuing other talents such as writing or art.

Young women's shifting relationships with female relatives and peers can make future planning tentative. Without people whom you can count on consistently, it becomes more difficult to plan the future. For some young

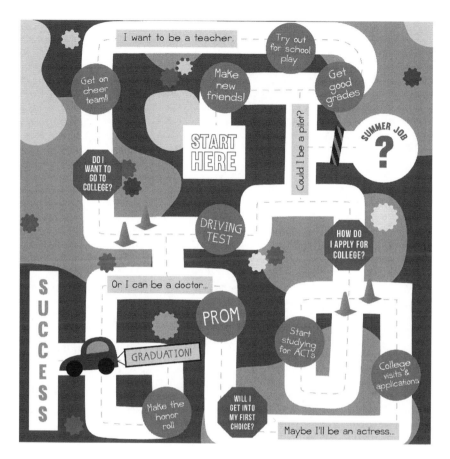

Figure 11.1 A young women's map

women, their changing constellation of friends, as well as often-difficult relationships with their parents, can make getting through the week seem like a tough plan to implement, never mind planning a few years ahead.

An example of a young women's map is shown in Figure 11.1.

Young Men's Maps

Young men, on the other hand, tend to make rather sparse maps. They may even structure their career around athletic seasons, rather than the rhythms of the academic year. They often have many fewer intermediate steps than girls, and whole years of information and steps can be missing in the middle of the map.

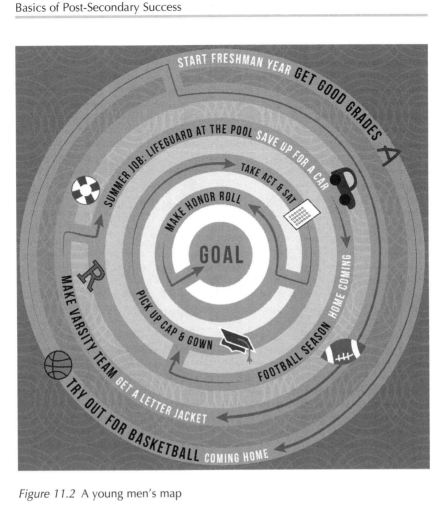

Figure 11.2 A young men's map

Young men also have not broadened their opportunities the way young women have. While young women have a wide range of careers to choose from (traditionally female to traditionally male), most young men have highly stereotypical notions of what men should do to earn a living. As sociologist Al Young (2004) has shown, many men in low-income neighborhoods look to hard work with one's hands as the standard of masculinity, at a time when that sort of work is on the decline. For many young men, looking to a future that involves a traditionally female role, such as a nurse, may not fit the image of what a man should be doing all day.

An example of a young men's map is shown in Figure 11.2.

What Should Go in a Map?

- **Ultimate destination**: where do they want to go? This can be a career or an educational path. The goal should be determined by the mapmaker.
- **Now**: where are they now? Where are they going to school? What activities are they involved in? What is their family like? All of these should go into the start of the map.
- **Intermediate goals**: what are steps along the way that they know they need to meet in order to move forward? For students aiming towards college, events that can go on the map include building a solid high school GPA, scoring well enough on standardized tests, going through the college search process, making the application, applying for financial aid, and seeking scholarships. For students aiming towards a career option, steps could include the skills needed, the training required, the experiences that will help confirm this choice (job shadowing, informational interviewing), and applying for a job.
- **Specific goals**: in many cases, young people just say their goal is "college," but this can be so universal as to be a cliché. Do they mean a two-year college, a four-year degree, or a career-certificate program? A mentor can ask some clarifying questions here to move the young person out of what they think is a socially acceptable answer to a real response.
- **Sources of help**: for key steps, students should come up with people from whom they can get help. In high school, this might be their mentor; in college, it might be a tutoring center, advisor, or success coach. But it helps students to realize that needing help will be inevitable for them as they enter a new college or a new career. They need to have some ideas about whom they might approach for help.

CONVERSATION STARTERS

— What do you really like to do in school?
— What activities do you love outside of school?
— What are things you really are good at, and enjoy doing?
— How do these line up to options after high school graduation?

When Youth Really Do Not Have Ideas

When I have young people about to map out a future, some of them do not take it well. When I did this exercise with our GEAR UP students, one just started to cry uncontrollably. She did not imagine that college was in her future, and could not think of anything else. The end of high school was like a cliff for this young woman, with nothing bridging the chasm. This is not a good moment to push young people even harder. Finding any goal that a young person might have is an important task for a mentor, even if that goal is rather modest in scope.

 TIE TO LEADERSHIP

The Teenager's Brain

Laurence Steinberg's 2014 book, *Age of opportunity: Lessons from the new science of adolescence*, makes some key points about changes in how we view teens.

First, Steinberg points out that adolescence is getting longer because puberty is beginning sooner in young people. Girls enter puberty now at an average of 9 years old, while boys do so at about 10½ years. On the other hand, adulthood is starting later, with many young people delaying marriage and leaving the family home in their mid-20s.

While this is not necessarily good news, as adolescence is a dangerous time of life for young people, it does create a window of opportunity. During this time, the human brain is highly "plastic" as it grows. This creates the opportunity to develop mentally at about the same quick rate as children do between birth and age 3. This gives mentoring programs for young people a real chance to positively influence them at a time when their brains are ready to use all that information and can get the most out of it.

However, science reveals a double-edged sword in this longer, more important adolescence. Given positive environments and positive people in their lives, young people can really thrive during this period, exiting it ready to be mature, self-sufficient adults. This plasticity however, makes their minds more vulnerable to things that make you feel good quickly—drugs and alcohol—and also more vulnerable to negative peer pressure, as well as more likely to experience mood disorders and mental illness.

Resources

Steinberg, L. D. (2014). *Age of opportunity: Lessons from the new science of adolescence.* Boston, MA: Houghton Mifflin Harcourt.

Young, A. A. (2004). *The minds of marginalized black men: Making sense of mobility, opportunity, and future life chances.* Princeton, NJ: Princeton University Press.

12 | Exposure to College Options and Choices

Students report that trips to visit colleges and workplaces are among the most powerful methods of inspiring them and informing them of their options. While funding and logistical issues hobble the ability for teachers to get youth out in the field, mentors and mentoring programs become even more critical in making sure these experiences happen. Given the cost and difficulty of these trips, mentors and program leaders should think carefully about how to best expose their students to higher education and career opportunities, and then connect it to their lives at school and in their neighborhood.

For trips, consider starting local. You should never assume that students have "already been there" when planning trips. When we started our GEAR UP program, we thought every student in Ypsilanti had been on my campus. (It would seem impossible to miss.) But over 20 percent of students had never set foot on a campus that might be a 10-minute walk or drive from their house. Many of those who had "been there" had probably never set foot in a building there. Even if young people have been on a campus for an event, how many have been on a campus tour? Talked to admissions counselors? Toured a working science lab? Attended a theatrical performance?

No college or workplace should be ruled out at the start of the process. We learned during our program that many students viewed our local community college with disdain, treating it as a school for losers. This reaction among 17-year olds was common, even as adults were pouring into the community college for focused, career-certificate programs in such areas as web design, culinary arts, and music production. Working to break down these stereotypes was important to help students see options where they could not recognize them.

⬌ REFLECTION

— What places did you visit as a child or teenager that made a real impact on your ideas about the future?

— What was it about the "power of the place" that prompted this?

To get the most out of trips, students need to be prepared—they need enough information to get started on a field trip. This may mean pre-teaching some key concepts, giving background information, or looking at a museum website before going. This does not need to be extensive, or make the trip redundant, but it helps for students to know the basics about a school or workplace before they get there, and know enough about how to behave for your program to get invited back.

It helps to give students some kind of activity during a trip to focus their attention on key details. This could be as simple as writing a few questions before the trip to ask when they get there. This might be a worksheet, though "scavenger hunt" activities do not always produce the best learning results. Taking photos of key sites and activities can be a good activity, as can taking notes for a future writing assignment. A word of warning: untethering students from their electronics can be a key to getting them to pay attention on a visit. If they are on their phones during a tour, they are really not taking a "trip" at all. They are just carrying their electronic cocoon from place to place.

When groups come to our campus, I make it a point to talk about such concepts as "grit" and "growth mindset" with them. They need to be able to see themselves as successful future college students in order to make it to campus. They need to be able to work hard, even when they are frustrated, if they are going to earn the test scores and grades they will need to go where they want for education or for a career. They need to be able to think of new strategies when they are struggling in class, and to know where to go to seek out help on campus, help that they will inevitably need. They need to know that there will come a time when they will need to rethink their strategy in a class or major—change the way they study, the way they write, the way they attend class—when the old way just does not seem to work.

This might sound like taking the fun out of the visit, but a college campus or career setting is not the zoo: the students are not just there to look at the animals. If they are going to learn something from visits and trips, those experiences need to help them on the path to where they are going.

After the trip, much of the educational value for students comes from talking about or writing about their experiences. This time for reflection is often cut in the desire to get done quickly, but it is the most important moment of the experience in many ways. Students should be writing or talking about what they learned on the trip and what questions they still might have. This reflection can work its way into the "thank you note" as well, for any adults that helped facilitate the trip. Sample prompts for students might include:

- What were some positive and negative aspects of the campus?
- Do you think this college/career program is a good fit for you?
- Did you meet other students like you who are successful there?
- How readily available does academic and other help seem to be?
- Do the programs you are interested in studying seem strong there?
- If you change your mind about your interests, are other programs strong as well?
- What opportunities for research, service, and leadership seem to exist in this program for students?
- Who gets opportunities at this college or workplace? Are undergraduates restricted to washing glassware at the lab? Are entry-level people ever promoted?

As you take students to more and more locations, get them to think in comparative terms about the places. As students see more than one campus or more than one career site, get them to compare and contrast each, even doing a quick Venn diagram with them. While this may seem basic, students have a sharp eye for similarities and differences of institutions and settings, and it helps to put this to work. The more they see, the better they will get at this, and when it comes time to make decisions about where they feel they fit, or where they feel they will learn the most, it is important that they have had practice making these comparisons with adult help.

In the course of a GEAR UP or Upward Bound program, students can really become sharp customers. Students I have worked with have discovered that some colleges claim to have excellent majors and programs in anything they might ask about. Even as high school students, they figured out that no college could possibly be so great at so many different things. While not helping to make them cynical, having discussions about the marketing messages of colleges, and how these align with reality, can help students begin to narrow their choices.

TIE TO LEADERSHIP

Over- and Under-Matching

Discussions with adults can help students avoid mismatch in the college admissions process. The Obama administration has taken on the issue of "under-matching," in which low-income students often pick schools that are nearby but are less academically rigorous than what they might have otherwise achieved. However, the flip side is that those who run programs for high school students are painfully aware of "bounce back," in which top students in their schools arrive home in the winter term of freshman year, often with several Fs in their classes, yet-to-be-paid tuition bills, and a desire to move home and attend a local college.

Helping students get to where they are going to thrive is a key responsibility of a mentor, and it is a tricky balance between challenging young people and setting them up for failure. The role of adults in this process is to help the young person think through the issue from numerous angles, and to come up with the best answer that he or she can right now.

 CONVERSATION STARTERS

— What colleges and universities would you want to visit if cost were no object?
— What workplaces would you want to spend a day in, if there were no limit on what you chose?

From the answers to these, it is almost always possible to come up with "something like" what the student has chosen as an idea.

Resource

Hoxby, C., & Turner, S. (2015). *What high-achieving low-income students know about college.* Cambridge, MA: National Bureau of Economic Research.

13 | Nuts and Bolts of College Application

College application is a marathon, not a sprint. Mentors are key to helping students understand their options, set realistic goals, and to pursue a reasonable number of possibilities for future success. This means working against some aspects of the current culture of college applications, and the way in which students have been encouraged to apply to an ever-lengthening list of schools in order to successfully enroll in a prestigious institution.

Before the Applications

Before applying to colleges or for other opportunities, students need to think carefully about the case they are able to make for themselves. For students interested in selective colleges and universities, even some state colleges and universities, they need to build a record in high school that helps them stand out. In many cases, having some real community service and leadership experience—and being able to explain why these are important—can be a critical edge.

Mentors can help students in high school think about the opportunities they have available to show service and leadership, and to make sure they are not passing by experiences that can set them apart from their peers. This does not always mean studying abroad or other resource-intensive activities. Students I interviewed at a local high school that faced financial challenges had organized to raise funds for basic school supplies for their teachers in the face of budget cuts. The way they took on a tough issue and pulled together was more impressive than many parent-orchestrated summer activities.

⬍ REFLECTION

— What was the process like when you applied to college?
— Which parts did you find easy? Which parts baffling?
— How has the process changed for your mentees?

An important part of the process of service and leadership involves reflection. Mentors can ask students to reflect on their service and leadership experiences, which will help them organize their thoughts when they write or talk about it. While many students know they should be doing something for their communities, or should consider being an officer for a club, very few seniors can explain how or why they showed leadership or service, or how it was important to them.

Calendar for Applications/Financial Aid

It is helpful to draw up a long-term plan with mentees around the college application process. The following can serve as a guide, with changes based on local circumstances.

Freshman/Sophomore Year

Freshman year is a pivotal year for high school and the first year that really counts for college admissions. From their first day of ninth grade, students are building a GPA that will, in a few years, unlock scholarship aid automatically at many colleges. The tests they take and the homework they turn in are earning them money towards their future goals. They also start learning material for testing that will form their ACT or SAT score. Mentees must be reminded that each piece of homework turned in, each test passed with an A or B, each project completed for a grade, will be worth money to them in just a few years. Sophomore year is often easier for students to handle than freshman year, but again, it is a time when students can earn good grades that will help them make the case for themselves as serious students.

Junior Year

This is a key year in terms of grades, as well as test scores. By this time, students should be taking the hardest classes they can successfully manage, hopefully some at the Advanced Placement or college level. While they are earning grades and studying for the SAT/ACT, this year is a key time to assess what colleges are of interest to them and the range of colleges to which they might apply.

Senior Year

This is not the time to get senioritis!

Fall: in the fall, applications are due very quickly – they should be in by October 31 in many cases. For selective schools, just about all students are better off applying early. For any college, applying on the early side gives time to get together needed documents, make sure all letters of recommendations and forms are in, and that transcripts of grades and test scores are sent.

Starting in 2016, October 1 will become the key moment to apply for financial aid by filling out the FAFSA (Free Application for Federal Student Aid, available at http://fafsa.ed.gov). Financial aid at almost all schools is first come, first served, and the options available by filing early are much more lucrative than those available in March and April. By April 15, the student's family needs to file a tax form for the year to support the FAFSA.

April/May: this is a key set of months to make decisions. First, acceptances, denials, and wait lists will come in. More important for many of our students, this is the time financial-aid award letters come in, and they need to be compared. Mentors can help compare packages, and get follow-up information from colleges about what they really cost.

May/June/July: this is a key period for mentors to help students make a decision about where to attend, and to initiate the processes of enrollment. This includes signing up for classes, getting an appointment with college advisors, and figuring out the student's living and food situations for the next year. Mentors can play a key role helping the student map out a series of deadlines for each of these transactions, and help prevent the "summer melt" that causes many low-income students to be accepted into college but fail to show up in September.

Filling Out Applications

In my time working with young people, and interviewing students for my alma mater, I have seen the number of applications, particularly to selective institutions, explode. When I was a senior in high school, I applied to five colleges, and at the time this seemed ambitious. This included a local state college that served as my safety school, a few institutions in nearby New York City, and a few colleges further away that had caught my eye.

This application process ate much of my senior year, between essays, retaking standardized tests to get higher scores, researching my options, and making a few visits with my mother to colleges. It was not until I visited one college and sat in on a class that I knew where I belonged. Many people in my generation and older faced a limited range of choices for college, and set some parameters around their search (cost, commute, distance from home, nearby relatives) that helped keep the field to a manageable number of schools.

Students today have a far wider range of choices, have access to more information, and are under pressure to apply to many more institutions, and many more selective institutions. As top colleges accept a smaller and smaller percentage, students need to apply to more and more institutions to have a chance at getting into one. The Common Application allows students to fill out one basic form, then add information, to apply for up to 20 schools. States have set up systems to make it easier for students to apply to multiple colleges with the click of a mouse.

Unfortunately, this new world does not always serve students well. As Stephanie Hawkes, an Upward Bound Program Specialist, put it, college needs to fit into the long-term plans of the student, not just another place to apply. Another Upward Bound Program Specialist, Haley Mulka, asks her students to apply to five colleges—no more—so that they can research their options thoroughly. Many times, students are attracted to colleges and majors based on superficial knowledge.

I have found that students in high school know less and less about where they are applying. While they know the names of all the top schools they feel they are supposed to apply to, they know little about what makes them distinctive, and as a result cannot make the case for their fit with the school. What are supposed to be alumni interviews with me asking questions can become an information session, in which I explain what stands out about the school and how it is different from other options.

Many times while interviewing students, I get the feeling from their halting answers that they have never been asked about their future plans, what they want to study, and why they really want to attend college. A mentor can be a valuable sounding board for students, asking valuable questions in advance of interviews and decisions, and getting students to start owning their own choices and decisions.

CONVERSATION STARTERS

Some good questions that students should think about before applying to college:

- What do you want to study in college?
- What careers interest you?
- What do you think will be hard about the first year of college?
- What transitions have you faced that are similar?
- Where have you shown service and leadership in high school?
- Do you plan to continue your high school activities in college or take up new ones?

Problems Students Have in the Process

Upward Bound personnel notice a few big problems that students have in the college application process. One is just running out of time and energy at key points. Students can take on more and more complex applications than they thought, and simply run out of time and energy to get everything completed. This is particularly true of essays, required by many colleges and many scholarship programs. Facing pressures of senior year classes and activities, many high school students simply run out of gas, and turn out poor or incomplete work that does little to highlight their strengths or explain the shortcomings in their high school records.

Faced with one more essay to write, many students can abandon colleges that might serve them well, or incredible scholarship opportunities for lack of between 250 and 500 good words. A student in Upward Bound abandoned a Gates Foundation Millennium Scholarship opportunity due to the writing involved.

Mentors can help here by encouraging writing, and even setting aside some time to help students write or revise essays well before application season starts. All students can work on a short but powerful personal statement that expresses their background and aspirations. Help from a caring adult can make sure that students neither understate their talents, nor underplay the barriers they have faced.

Students have trouble getting all materials together for applications, including transcripts, letters, essays, and other paperwork. Mentors can help students get organized, and can help them set up a schedule for junior and senior year.

Rethinking the Process: Senior Year into College Mentoring

For many mentors (and parents) high school graduation is an end point, indicating that their work with a young person has been a success. However, a lot can happen in the period between college acceptance and enrollment in September, almost all of it negative. Mentors and mentoring programs can provide critical support in this time period, when many times support from teachers and guidance counselors comes to an end.

The Challenge of Enrollment

Once a student is accepted into college, and a financial-aid package is in place, there are still a whole series of important steps that students must take to actually enroll. Many colleges simply send students an email with their new college email account, and then begin communicating exclusively through it. Making sure that students are in contact with their college in the spring of senior year can be a critical step to getting to the new campus in September.

Deposits and Contracts

Depending on where a student will live and eat, there are a whole series of deposits and contracts due to a college. This can be minimal, but even in the case of community colleges, missing a deadline for a deposit can set a student back to square one. A mentor's reminders, help in planning, and advocacy, can help in these situations.

Senior Year Grades

Traditionally, the senior year in America is one vast conspiracy against a strong academic finish for students. A series of time-consuming and costly events (prom, graduation parties) keep students' focus off their classes and their final exams. As the year wraps up, disciplinary problems and pranks can distract from the important business of finishing with a strong GPA and all required classes/credits required for graduation. Despite what students think, colleges can place students on academic probation in the fall, or revoke their invitations, if the senior year experience wraps up unsuccessfully. Mentors can help keep students focused and keep them from getting sucked up into senior year drama.

Looking Ahead to College with Mentees

Students after graduation, despite what they think, are not yet independent adults. Over the past generation, we have gradually extended adolescence in our society. Where we once thought people at age 21 were ready to have a self-supporting job, be married, and perhaps starting a family, we now think of 26 as the end of adolescence and start of adulthood. Therefore, when students leave mentoring relationships or programs at the end of high school, we need to be able to help them find the resources they will need for the next stage of their lives.

There are a few critical areas where a mentor can assist in the college "handoff." Are there support programs on campus from which this student will need to receive support in order to be successful? Think about contacting these offices, getting your mentee to contact them, or going together to meet someone there. The following is a short list of places to get help—not meant to limit, but to encourage.

- All students will run into academic trouble in at least one class. Does the student know where the campus tutoring center is?
- College students are among the worst at taking physical care of themselves. Does the student know where campus or off-campus health resources are and how to access them? This might be an on-campus health center or an off-campus clinic that focuses on adolescent health. Does the student know how to call and make an appointment for herself or himself at a health center?

- Almost all students will face stress, and perhaps mental illness, at some time in college, or have a close friend who does so. Does the student know about campus counseling resources?
- Are there mentoring, outreach, or support programs at the new location? Are there key individuals who are known to "look out for" students who may need extra guidance? Are there initiatives at the new location that are looking for students such as the one you are mentoring? Some research and some phone calls/emails can sometimes locate amazing resources and help for young people.
- Are there simple things you can buy to help your student get started? Sometimes items such as extra-long sheets can be a barrier to getting to a dorm. A full set of move-in or bathroom supplies can be of help to allow your student to fit in with more affluent peers. Even a coffee-shop gift card can help out for the first set of midterms.

Warning: You May Not Be Done Mentoring

Just as many parents have found that they still have a substantial parental job while their children are in their 20s, mentors can find out that just because a student has entered college, their job may not be done. If you are willing to go the distance, you can help your mentee make a good transition to college, recover from freshman year missteps, and begin the journey to a meaningful college and work career. You can also help steer your student to continue with community service while in college, and to consider becoming a mentor herself or himself. This type of service can help students see meaning in their own education, can help them see themselves as a potential role model, and can aid in college persistence and retention.

 TIE TO LEADERSHIP

Who Applies to College Based on Their Family?

Researcher Kassie Freeman, in her book, *African-Americans and college choice* (2005), puts family expectations at the center of how students choose whether to attend college and where to attend. Some students ("knowers") are in families that assume that they will go on to higher education. Other students ("seekers") are in families that did not attend college, but still encourage their young people to go beyond the family level of education (to serve as a role model for other young people in the family, for instance.) Finally, there are young people ("dreamers") who decide to attain college just from seeing negative role models in their lives, people who could have gone on to further education but missed the chance, limiting their opportunities. In terms of mentoring programs, "knowers" only need help in choosing which college makes sense; "seekers" need help navigating the process, but are highly motivated by their families; and "dreamers" often start late in the process and need the most assistance in making it through the process.

In *Choosing colleges*, Patricia McDonough (1997) makes the case that schools shape whether students seek to attend college, where they apply, and where they attend. McDonough looks at guidance offices. She found that higher SES schools encouraged a wide range of college choices (in terms of selectivity and geography), while low SES schools lacked the resources to help students beyond local college choices. Given the bleak portrait in McDonough's book, mentoring programs would need to provide working-class and lower-income students with almost all the information about attending colleges not in the local area, and provide help from arranging visits to preparing application materials to applying for financial aid and scholarships.

Resources

Freeman, K. (2005). *African-Americans and college choice: The influence of family and school.* Albany: State University of New York Press.

McDonough, P. M. (1997). *Choosing colleges: How social class and schools structure opportunity.* Albany: State University of New York Press.

College Aspirations and Affordability

Young People and Financial Aid

Barriers to Paying for College

When students and their families are on a college tour looking at colleges today, they are often thinking about whether it is attainable ("Do they let students like me in?") as well as affordable ("Can my family pay for this?"). As tuition and other charges have increased, and as student and parent debt has ballooned, finances become more important to college decisions, not less. This is a major shift from when many mentors attended college. Institutions (particularly state institutions) were more affordable then, tuition was less of a burden on families, and loans were a way to close gaps in aid— they were not the majority of assistance offered.

Students face many barriers in paying for college, and only some can be addressed by mentors. While mentors can certainly encourage students to shop widely for a college, and help families get an early start on the FAFSA (Free Application for Federal Student Aid), there are limits to what any caring adult can do in this situation.

 REFLECTION

— How did your family pay for college?
— How much did you have to work? Borrow?

This may come as a shock to adult mentors, as the loan debt that a student might previously have acquired in four years of college is now the amount that a student might borrow per year.

Hurdle 1: Sticker Shock

University of Michigan financial-aid expert Jim Eddy points to the sticker price of college as the biggest barrier he sees students facing. First-generation students and their families often do not take into account that many schools have high tuitions, but also have the resources to offer generous aid to lower-income families, making them more affordable than an institution with a seemingly lower price. Students and families shopping for a college face a series of hurdles, and the first is unique to higher education. Unlike buying a good like a television or refrigerator, purchasers of higher education face a market where the price on the product differs widely for many of those involved. In some cases, most attending receive some form of aid or discount rather than paying the full "list price."

But this process is opaque and serves low-income and first-generation students and families poorly. Rather than being able to see whether they can afford a college or university, they can only see, on a web page, what they seemingly cannot afford. Ironically, some institutions that are best placed to help low-income students afford college have the most out-of-sight list prices imaginable, thus scaring off potential students.

All colleges and universities are required to post a "net price calculator" on their website. These include information on tuition and fees, room and board, and the average cost of attendance for students depending on family income. However, this system has some bugs, and it can overstate the cost of attendance for low-income students by significant amounts.

Focusing in on a few key schools, and digging deep into how to afford them, can pay off. Looking at a handful of schools gives students the chance to look at special programs or scholarships for students in their position, and will give a better sense of what aid might be available. Both admissions and financial-aid personnel at universities are used to these questions and are often eager to highlight what they can offer.

Hurdle 2: Avoiding Scams

At all points in the application and financial-aid process, I would suggest mentoring students towards institutions that have a good track record of helping low-income students and do not have a record for exploiting their students. Higher education is less regulated than one might think, and many for-profit and unethical non-profit providers are out there, looking for federal Pell Grant money and student loan dollars.

Proprietary schools that draw an overwhelming amount of their income from the federal government are placed on the US Department of Education's list of 90/10 institutions. This can give you a snapshot of how programs are financed, and if they seem like they are drawing much more money from the federal government than from their own students, you may want to question your choice. Similarly, private institutions that offer quick paths into business, health care, and other hot fields are often far more expensive than the community college and public university alternatives. This is another place to have a discussion about whether this is the right move for the mentee.

Last year, during college application week, we were helping a young man look for an auto mechanics trade school near Houston, where he planned to relocate. The only option he could find online was a proprietary school that had no application available online. He was required to come in to the school to learn more about it. This method is about the same used to sell time-shares, and it was a red flag about this being a wise investment of his time and money.

You are not crushing a young person's dreams when you ask whether their choice of school will deal with them in an ethical manner. Good, ethical institutions will show caring and concern for students throughout the process—from admissions, to financial aid, to advising, to the classroom. If the student is not seeing this in one area of a college or university, it is a clear sign that the institution may not be a good choice.

Hurdle 3: The Dreaded FAFSA

While the federal government has worked to simplify the FAFSA, it can still be a major hurdle for students. Their family needs to fill out the FAFSA online early in January, then file tax forms by April 15. The family will then receive a statement of financial aid from each school to which the student has applied. Unfortunately, this aid letter can be misleading. The school may present aid in unfamiliar categories, or the school may offer more aid to first-year students than to later classes. Many students and families need help in navigating this process, because attending a school that a student cannot afford is a recipe for failure.

Colleges face many situations in which they feel that families are hiding assets and income. Given their clientele, they are often correct about high-income families' understanding their assets and income. As a result, financial-aid offices are often set up to be miniature detective agencies. They become suspicious of any family that seems to lack the income or assets of their peers. For actual low-income students and families, this can make an embarrassing situation completely humiliating, as families are forced to prove that they are as poor as they say that they are.

If you have genuine concern about young people attending and staying in college, get ready to go to a meeting with financial aid with them to discuss the situation. While people in the field of financial aid can be pessimistic in their view of human nature, the appearance of an adult mentor in the office can turn around the situation. While sitting in the financial-aid office I have seen opportunities open up that were not offered any other way, allowing students a fighting chance of enrolling in and successfully completing college.

Long-Term Hurdle: Minimizing Debt

When students and families receive a financial-aid award letter, they need to spend time looking at the breakdown of their package. Programs can help young people and their parents understand that not all financial aid is created equal. At the top of the scale are **grants**, which are aid dollars that do not need to be paid back. Students will need to look at the requirements to receive and to renew these grants, as many will require a number of credits taken and passed. This may also include a GPA requirement to renew.

Next on the list is **work-study**, in which a college grants a sum of money to be earned at an on-campus job. These are also high-quality awards, as long as the student can find a job on campus and thus access the money. In addition, a good work-study job will include adults in the office who can serve as mentors to help the student navigate his or her first year on campus.

The biggest difference between college now and college a decade ago is the role of **student loans**. The number of loans that students and parents take out has increased greatly over the years, and the sources of those loans have changed to include more private loans. While loans are a good source of funding for college, they can be dangerous, as they can never be discharged, even in bankruptcy. Many young people could find student loan debt following them into retirement and their social security garnished to help pay off mistakes made decades ago. Right now, two out of three students will graduate with student loan debt, with an average of more than $29,000. Low-income students often borrow more to pay for the shortfall between what their parents are told to pay (expected family contribution) and what they realistically can provide.

Hidden Cost: Remedial Classes

For many students looking towards college, math and other requirements can derail the process of earning credits towards a degree. In Michigan, about 50,000 students go from high school to college, but over 10,000 of these students find themselves taking remedial math coursework. In many cases, this means that they are in college but doing the same work they have seen (and failed to master) in high school. Reading and writing skills can also land students in remedial classes as well, giving Michigan an average of more than 27 percent of students attending college but not yet taking college-level work.

If you break down that total into groups, the numbers become even more disturbing. For African-American students, most (52 percent) will be starting college with at least one remedial class. Proportions are high for other groups as well: students with disabilities (55 percent), English-language learners (48 percent), homeless students (44 percent), and students from disadvantaged backgrounds (41 percent) (all statistics found at www.mischooldata.org).

A lot of hard work has been done at the high school level to help more students access college. This includes such programs as Upward Bound, GEAR UP, College Advising Corps, mentoring programs, and Promise Scholarships. But if the students entering college are trapped in remedial coursework, they are not really attending college. They are often paying to take classes that do not count towards their degree, often using up federal financial-aid eligibility, and perhaps even taking out loans to do so.

The placement testing and remediation system means that many students are closer to graduating from college before they enroll and take a placement exam than after, as remediation can add several classes to the 40 or so needed to graduate. These students are then placed into classes they have been less successful at in the past, and are unable to take the classes in their major or elsewhere in the curriculum that have the potential to really affect their thinking, build skills, and open new horizons for them.

For mentors and mentoring programs, getting students over this hurdle is a key to helping them really thrive in college. Throughout middle and high school, a consistent message that skills in math, reading, and writing really count in the long term is a must. Mastering the content of such areas as arithmetic, algebra, geometry, and trigonometry is not glamorous, but I often tell students that if they did not like taking these classes in high school, for free, with textbooks provided free of charge, they are going to like it less a few years from now, paying for the course.

Mentors can help students "eat the frog," or take on the most challenging tasks of college first, rather than wait for their senior year to start their math requirement. For many of my students in college, passing the math requirement is like jumping over the Berlin Wall. It is often the very last requirement students tackle in senior year, and they simply make a run for it, hoping to make it to graduation successfully.

As students are transitioning to college enrollment, mentors can play a key role by making sure students get to campus prepared to take placement exams. This might involve spending time freshening up their skills (Khan Academy is a great resource for this) or just developing some strategies to take the test itself. Students struggle more when they put off taking placement tests, or put off taking required math and English courses, so encouraging them to take these subjects early in their college careers can be helpful as well.

Last Hurdle: Scholarships

Many students think of applying for scholarships as an optional part of the college application process, something to do if they have time left over. This is a big mistake, as the money scholarships provide can make a real difference in the quality of life of students and parents. Encouraging students to write a resume and the essays in advance is vital for both college and scholarship applications. For my family, a few scholarships from my high school and my father's union provided money for last-minute items I needed to go away to school.

👥 REAL PEOPLE

Haley Mulka has worked as a program specialist at Upward Bound and insists that her students apply for as many scholarships as they are eligible. The follow through of students varies from year to year, but Mulka has had classes of Upward Bound students (10–15 per year) earn over $500,000 in scholarships towards their education, through sheer persistence and hard work.

It is now common for our office to learn that scholarships, even free rides, go unclaimed at colleges and universities. These are not just specialized programs for obscure groups, but full tuition at community colleges in our community. Students need to be on the lookout for anything they might be eligible for: leadership scholarships, service scholarships, and academic scholarships.

Students fail to realize that from senior year of high school on into college (until graduation), they need to build a radar system to look for and apply for any scholarship they can find. At the high school level, this might mean local service groups and clubs, and once in college, looking for offices and departments that offer aid. All the way through college graduation, students should be scanning their college and other websites for scholarship opportunities and then applying for those for which they are eligible.

What Happens When Parents Will Not Pay for College

One of the most dispiriting issues for mentors to encounter is students who desperately want to attend college, with parents who refuse to pay. This can come from a situation involving divorce, it can result from a child coming out of the closet as gay or lesbian, or it can come from a belief by the parent that the child is old enough to fend for himself or herself.

While there is seldom an ideal solution for the situation, I always look to the financial-aid office involved for help. Most professionals in the field have seen a wide range of family meltdowns, and in some cases, students can document estrangement from their family and become classified as "independent" students. Even if they are not eligible for this, there are tools that financial-aid offices can use to help make up the gap that students face.

 TIE TO LEADERSHIP

The research on financial aid and families shows that if aid is targeted to students who need it, if it is clear how to access it, and if families are helped in the application process, students are more likely to attend college, are more likely to finish college, and are more likely to make progress steadily towards a degree. When Castleman and Long (2013) looked at students in Florida who received a need-based scholarship based on grade and test scores, this made it more likely for those students awarded grants to attend and complete college than their peers who did not.

Removing financial barriers can make a difference for students. A study showed that if parents received help on the FAFSA at the same time they went to H&R Block to do their taxes, the students in the family were more likely to apply to and enroll in college the next year (Bettinger, Long, Oreopoulos, & Sanbonmatsu, 2009).

Programs that work to reduce the barriers that families face to financing college can make a major positive difference. If your program can spare resources to help students with scholarship applications, FAFSA completion, or just help parents understand the financial-aid process, more students will be able to attend and complete college, and will finish with less debt than their peers.

Resources

Bettinger, E., Long, B. T., Oreopoulos, P., & Sanbonmatsu, L. (2009). *The role of simplification and information in college decisions: Results from the H&R Block FAFSA experiment.* Cambridge, MA: National Bureau of Economic Research.

Castleman, B. L., & Long, B. T. (2013). *Looking beyond enrollment: The causal effect of need-based grants on college access, persistence, and graduation.* Cambridge, MA: National Bureau of Economic Research.

For information on proprietary schools and their sources of income, see http://studentaid.ed.gov/about/data-center/school/proprietary

The US Department of Education's college cost calculator is found at www.collegecost.ed.gov/catc/#

When College Is Not the Right Choice Right Now

Non-College Options

Not every student is ready to commit to attending college, and college is not the best choice for every student. Lumina Foundation CEO Jamie Merisotis (2015) has written that our definition of "college" needs opening up to consider a wider range of options. He argues:

> Our current system of postsecondary education is filled with a myriad of high-quality pathways to the American Dream, including technical-training certifications, apprenticeships, employer-based workforce-readiness programs, web-developer "boot-camps," and many more credentials that go far beyond the traditional two- and four-year degrees.

This resonates with anyone who worked in a program that defines only four-year college completion as success, even when it does not meet the needs of the student or support her or his family.

For many young people, a four-year degree, right now, is not a realistic option or one likely to lead to success. Think through the following cases.

1. A young man who lost his father to violence is committed to supporting his terminally ill mother and his siblings, and thus is unable to commit to college full-time. Does taking on such a level of responsibility make him a "failure" if he looks for work rather than a college?
2. A student needs to work more to support his young child. While taking on responsibilities as a father will interfere with college, is it right to try to talk him out of doing what he views as the right thing for his new family?

3. A student is just burned out from an unengaging high school curriculum that was highly academic and contained little connection to the real-world problems he was interested in addressing. Is work at a two-year college on a more applied and vocational degree a mistake?

Helping Young People Launch a Career after High School

Many education writers assume that once students finish their formal education, they should be able to pick up a career and go from there. Most continuations of education end with a career—K–career or cradle-to-career, for instance—indicating that career is the finish line for students.

Young people, though, do not always move in the straight lines that we expect them to, and often require more help even when they do reach the level we hope for. The job/career market for young people is a turbulent place, and many factors can displace young people from even good, stable jobs, back into the uncertain labor market.

 REAL PEOPLE

Melissa Calabrese

The skills that young people need to successfully navigate a path to college are the same as the skills they may need to find and keep a good job. Melissa Calabrese has worked with many young people who want to go to college eventually, but find themselves working to support a family. She finds that in order to be successful, most young people need to work on "soft skills" that allow them to succeed in the workplace. Being able to communicate with coworkers, having emotional intelligence in the workplace, and being able to use the resources available at work to advance are key challenges that many young people face.

When working with young people who want to go directly into a workplace, she looks for companies that will really support their employees and will provide opportunities to learn more and to advance. For many young people, college or community college may be a long-term aspiration, but there are some short-term goals—such as earning a commercial driver's license—that can make a real difference in being able to move up in an organization.

Young people looking for a job or a short-term educational opportunity after high school face a different task than students applying to colleges and universities for a four-year degree. If students are looking for a vocational program, a certificate, an apprenticeship, or a career-focused two-year degree, they are conducting something closer to a job search than a college application process. Like a job search, they only need to find one genuine opportunity, and then gain admission. The United States is rich in higher education resources, and there are enough colleges and universities in any area to provide a good experience for all students who are applying. But finding an ethical, effective program that teaches culinary arts or welding is a much more focused search, and you may be lucky to locate two or three good candidates within an hour's drive of the student's residence.

Building a Future Resume

For many programs, the desire to help students think about college and a career go hand and hand. Mark Jackson, when head of EMU's Upward Bound, developed a "future resume" activity, which challenged students to think about their resume a few years in the future (graduating high school or college), fill in the information they already knew, and fill in the rest with what they aspired to: education, skills, organizations joined. Then he challenged the students to think of the next steps to fill in the gaps that they could see in front of them. This activity also encourages participants in your program to have an up-to-date resume always available, often needed on short notice when education, job, or internship opportunities appear.

The Role of Community Colleges

Community colleges—institutions that focus on applied and vocational two-year and certificate programs—are an underutilized resource in American education. When I was graduating from Sachem North High School, the local community college was nicknamed "Sachem North North" to indicate its lack of status and its role as a continuation of high school.

Among young people, particularly in low-income communities, this stigma against community college persists, even though adults flock to the low-cost, high-demand programs that they offer. At a recent College Decision Day I attended, the assembled students laughed when they saw the number attending the local community college, while their parents, aunts, and uncles are signing up for classes in web design, coding, entrepreneurship, and culinary arts at the same institution.

Most high school students have little idea of what is offered at community colleges. In part, this is because so many vocational programs that introduced students to these fields have been cut, leaving students in an almost entirely academic program, even when they crave more hands-on fields. Students also think of community college in terms of two-year degrees or transfer programs, often missing such fields as culinary arts, music production, and automotive technology programs. Community colleges have also been at the forefront of skilled trades and advanced manufacturing programs, offering apprenticeships and programs in such areas as welding, HVAC (heating, ventilation, air conditioning), electrical, green energy, and smart transportation.

Helping students understand the range of opportunities at community colleges, and getting them to understand their importance in worker training and retraining, will help them make informed decisions, particularly about cost. Community colleges offer many of the same programs offered at private, for-profit vocational institutions, at a fraction of the cost, and often with a much higher level of ethics.

 ## TIE TO LEADERSHIP

Relative Cost and Benefits of College

Economists have spent decades calculating how college pays off for students (or fails to). As the federal government and states have collected more data on colleges and employment, it has become easier to see that some relatively low-cost paths pay off quite well. Associate's Degrees (two-year degrees), particularly technical or science degrees offered by community colleges, often pay higher first-year salaries than many bachelor's programs (four-year degrees) (Cappelli, 2015). Certificate programs, particularly those between one and two years long, also launch students into areas with starting salaries above $30,000, without the time investment of a longer college program.

For Students Thinking About the Military

In many schools, particularly those in working-class or low-income areas, high school students may be thinking about a career in the armed services as a way to advance their career. This can have many different motivations. For some young people, military service runs deep in their family history, and they may want to keep up the tradition. For many others, though, the draws include the promise of adventure, travel, training, and funding for future education.

 REAL PEOPLE

Michael Wise

Michael Wise, an Army veteran who was a military recruiter, told me that for many students coming out of high school, the military can be an attractive option, particularly given the educational and other benefits of service. For Wise, after 12 years of elementary and secondary school, going to college immediately meant that he arrived on campus as "immature and irresponsible." Wise points out that "for many students just leaving high school, time in the service would provide responsibility, leadership, being part of a team, and the ability to live independently—with housing and salary provided."

However, the military is an option taken by fewer and fewer young people. About 1 percent of Americans have been in the service, and in many families, parents are fearful of what deployment can bring. Wise stresses that for many young people, service in the military can be a "viable choice, payoff for the future, and open many doors," but that parents need to be able to accept the risk of their children serving. However, to Wise, the military can help students obtain needed educational benefits and help pay for college (through the armed services, National Guard), as well as give them the skills and sense of responsibility to better pursue that education after their service is over.

Resources

Cappelli, P. (2015). *Will college pay off? A guide to the most important financial decision you'll ever make.* New York: Public Affairs.

Merisotis, J. (2015). *A new debate about "college."* www.luminafoundation.org/news-and-events/a-new-debate-about-college

4

Mentoring over the Long Haul

Hang in There!

Mentoring Through Crises in Young People's Lives

You get a call that a top student in your mentoring program is in trouble with the police—relatively big trouble, not just shoplifting.

The situation is disconcerting. This is a student who is held up as a role model in your program and has even taken on some responsibilities working with younger children. He has a clean disciplinary record in his high school, and you were looking forward to seeing him walk at high school graduation and head off to college this summer.

Do you give up?

 REFLECTION

— What are examples of times when caring adults in your life refused to give up on you, even when, looking back, you probably deserved it?

— What are cases where adults did not stick with you?

When Mentees Find Trouble, or Trouble Finds Them

What do you do when mentees get into trouble that they cannot fix on their own?

This is where things get tricky for mentors. As a general rule, mentors need to have strong boundaries and be able to view the situation objectively. A mentor is not a parent and needs to have a different approach. While a mentor aims to keep young people out of trouble and on the path to success, they cannot do so:

- without the mentee's permission
- without taking into account what the mentee wants and needs
- without removing the responsibility for the mentees' actions.

This means that, even in tough situations, mentors should not be coordinating the situation without the mentee's knowledge, doing what the mentor thinks is most important, and getting the mentee off the hook without responsibility. If a mentor does this, he or she is little more than the *deus ex machina* in a bad movie, manipulating the plot and ensuring that the mentee learns absolutely nothing from the situation.

In my years of teaching middle school, I saw situations where parents, for all the right reasons, tried to help their students out of multiple situations—college failure, poor grades, fighting, drug or alcohol abuse—without consequence for the young person who got into the trouble. I have watched this unfold over a decade since they left me in middle school, children whose parents did not expect their children to pay a price, even a small copayment, for their actions. Some have become non-adults, people in their 20s who are stalled in their careers as well as their lives.

Some Exceptions to This Rule

There are some situations in which a mentor simply needs to act to help a mentee, even if it seems to step over a line. The first is when a mentee is in danger of hurting himself or herself or others, or is in danger of being hurt. We have to train all our staff in the rules of what to do when young people disclose something either self- or other-harming.

In the case of potential suicide, contacting emergency services (911) is the critical step, particularly if the young person indicates that he or she has a plan for suicide.

If self-harm is indicated, but not as urgently, we have often been able to work with a school social worker or counselor to defuse the situation.

If young people are being abused—physically, sexually, or being neglected—the state child and family services office must be contacted. Many of us (teachers, counselors) are mandated reporters under state law and simply have no choice but to immediately report abuse and neglect cases.

When youth find themselves in trouble with law enforcement, mentors may need to take a more active role in digging them out of their own problems.

A young person's first negative contact with law enforcement is a critical step in his or her life, and it can influence his or her life forever. Mentors can serve as key advocates for young people, and may be able to help their mentee find their way to a diversion or other specialized program that can prevent the young person from moving deeper into the criminal justice system.

Questions to Ask About a Mentee in Trouble

How much of this action is caused by the mentee? There is a big difference between situations where a person is just the victim of an accident (hit by a car, punched at random), and situations where a mentee has really brought problems onto him or herself. In many of the communities where our mentees live, wrong place/wrong time is a way of life, and just being on the wrong corner at the wrong moment can lead to serious injury.

On the other hand, many times young people are at least the partial author of their own problems and need to face some consequence for it, or at least learn something from the experience. A mentor can help a mentee sort this out.

How serious is the problem? In some cases, the issue is critical. The mentee may face an overwhelming family crisis, a medical problem, a breakdown of mental stability, or contact with the police. In other cases, the consequences of the situation may be temporarily uncomfortable, but the long-term seriousness may be small. In the first set of circumstances, intervention and help by a mentor may be of the highest importance in keeping the young person stable and on the right path. In the second case, the mentee may be better off handling the situation and taking responsibility on his or her own.

What can the mentee learn from the situation? At the center of the mentor/mentee relationship is learning. It should be OK for mentees to fail and to admit failure to their mentor. Then the mentor can help unpack what the mentee has learned and how to avoid the same problem in the future. There are some places where more learning is possible than others, and some cases where the only lesson is not to do the same thing again.

CONVERSATION STARTERS

— What is happening right now in your life that is leading you to act like this? Tell me about your thinking.
— What consequences do you think your action/attitudes might have in the short term? Long term?

When to End a Mentoring Relationship

Mentoring is based on trust and on long-term commitment. When a young person is not responding to the current mentoring relationship or program, some hard questions need to be asked.

Is this the right relationship/program for the youth? Some young people may need a more intensive form of help than a mentoring program. Mentors cannot serve the role of mental-health professionals, such as psychologists or social workers. Knowing good referral sites for participants who need deeper or more intensive help is important for mentors to know and be able to facilitate.

Is this mentee committed to the program? All young people waiver in commitment, but if a mentee does not seem able to show up, is unable to follow program rules, or is disruptive, this means a conversation about the level of commitment needed. Youth rise to high expectations, so setting a high bar of commitment is important for programs and for mentors.

Has the relationship outlived its usefulness? Sometimes young people may "age out" of a mentoring program. They may find the relationship too prescriptive, and they may no longer value the activities. They may feel they have "heard it all" and absorbed all that the curriculum has to offer. My own daughter got a tremendous amount from the Girls on the Run curriculum the first time she went through it, and much less the second time. Like a sitcom, many programs are stale once they are in "repeats."

Rather than feel defensive when young people outgrow what you are doing, it pays to know the programs for the ages/stages right above yours, and to refer participants to those experiences. Or students who seem to be getting edgy and bored can move into leadership roles in your organizations, lead small groups, serve as a peer mentor, or be a presenter of key topics.

The Real Costs of Being a Mentor

Being a good mentor can be a bad career move. When you really try to advocate for young people, not every adult will respect your involvement. In such systems as the K–12 educational system, health system, or criminal justice system, there is an expectation that adults are all on the same page, and in some cases that means that adults are expected to close ranks.

When I have advocated for young people at the school where I was a teacher, I sometimes faced a serious backlash, especially when asking for one more chance for a kid who had caused trouble over the years. There is really no way around this. All you can do is to hold your ground and stick to your guns in the process. Colleagues of mine have faced public attack over writing letters of support for young people when they faced criminal charges for their actions, even though this is exactly what a mentor should do.

 TIE TO LEADERSHIP

Pipelines

The term "school-to-prison pipeline" has become much more commonly used now than a few years ago. The concept challenges us to think of school discipline helping lead young men—particularly young men of color—into a whirlpool of consequences that ends with state prison. I do not think the term is entirely fair or accurate, as those I know in schools and law enforcement are often heartbroken by the consequences that young people's actions can bring about from the criminal justice system.

Mentoring programs are a powerful tool to fight this pipeline effect and to pull youth off the path to prison. This can be done by helping young people stay out of trouble in the first place, taking them out of the path of trouble if they get onto it, or trying to turn them around once they fall into bad company.

Research has shown that juvenile diversion programs, which pair middle and high school students who have made their way to juvenile court with college students for mentoring activities, can have an amazing impact. One program has more than a 90 percent success rate in keeping youth from reoffending. Jennifer Kellman-Fritz, who runs the program at Eastern Michigan

University, works closely with the courts to make sure that the teenagers get all the services and help they need, in the hopes that this can head off future trouble.

This activity can help young people live much better lives as adults. Juvenile records are sealed and destroyed when a child reaches age 18 (unless charged as an adult), but criminal records can stand in the way of college enrollment, rule one out of financial aid, keep a person from working or finding an apartment, and haunt an adult for years.

If young people want to enter such fields as education, even a relatively minor crime, such as being a minor in possession of alcohol (e.g., drinking wine on your stoop before the age of 21), can make it difficult to start your career or even finish your training.

Not every teen can be convinced to stop breaking the rules. Many young people end up in trouble simply by being in the wrong place at the wrong time. Police and the courts can interpret the lack of judgment of young people as signs of criminal intent. Not every kid's problems are amenable to mentoring, especially when it comes to following the rules of school and the laws of the state. But mentoring programs have shown themselves effective in this area of stopping the problems of school discipline and juvenile court from becoming life-altering experiences for young people.

Resource

Bahena, S. (2012). *Disrupting the school-to-prison pipeline.* Cambridge, MA: Harvard Educational Review.

When Mentoring Relationships Change

Finding Ways to Mark Milestones in a Mentoring Relationship

Mentoring is tough work. It may require many hours of listening to young people to make sense out of what they want to do, and much time trying to formulate the right questions to get young people to think even a little differently about their paths.

Given the difficulty of this task, it is important to find ways to actively celebrate the successes, even small, which happen in a mentoring program, or even just between a mentor and a student. In some cases, just the persistence of the relationship is a reason to celebrate. As many young people have turbulent lives, actively reaching out and keeping in contact indeed merits celebration.

Celebrations of Community Investment in Young People

Young people rise to expectations, and food is no exception to this rule. In our program for young men, we tried to find one occasion to take them out to a sit-down restaurant each session. In one case, Alejandro Baldwin arranged for the young men to go to Seldom Blues, a restaurant on the Detroit riverfront. While we were ordering, a waiter at the restaurant taught the young men the basics of business lunch etiquette.

These kinds of celebrations are self-fulfilling prophesies. As young people feel more invested in by adults, they respond with positivity. As they feel more welcome in programs, they are more likely to respond to the program in positive ways.

Upward Bound programs feature such celebrations as banquets and graduations to help young people see the fruits of their hard work. Students in Upward Bound might attend a family banquet to celebrate the successful end of the school year, and a graduation ceremony to mark their successful completion of high school and acceptance into college.

Ways to Encourage Mentors and Mentees

Mentors can become discouraged, particularly when their mentees are floundering in the program, in school, or in life. Program leaders initiating discussion about what is going on can help keep mentors in the program and their energy levels up. Most adult mentors understand the need for long-term commitment but even the most dedicated individuals can feel that they are not being heard, or just feel useless given the problems that they face.

Good programs build in events and milestones that show both mentees and mentors their progress. This progress can be modest, such as staying out of trouble, or even getting into less trouble than could have been possible. Many mentoring programs for court-referred young people measure success by lack of recidivism and look to keep youth away from the juvenile justice system. Keeping a young person out of state prison, while not the highest goal imaginable, is still an achievement, and should be celebrated as much as acceptance to college.

Transition in Mentoring Relationships

Mentoring relationships do not remain the same. The relationships that people have with students in middle school are different from those they can have in high school, which is different from working with people as young adults, in college or not. At any age or grade level, mentors must be able to allow the relationships to shift depending on the needs of the mentee.

This is particularly true as young people become more conscious of their own status becoming adults, and less likely to accept directive advice. While in middle school, many young people are still willing to listen to adults because they are older, but as they mature they become more questioning of what they are told, even by people trusted in their lives.

For adult mentors, this means that more of their work with mentees might consist of questions, designed to help the young person think about his or her circumstances, or sharing incidents from his or her own life that may shed some light on the problems. This can be tricky, as teenagers have very strong "preachiness" detectors and can be resistant to even very solid advice.

As the relationship matures, mentoring relationships move closer to equality, since the young person gradually gains enough experience and insight to carry close to half of the conversation. As the relationship moves closer to equality, it may pay to close the mentor chapter of the relationship and allow it to move on to something else.

Ways to Mark "Graduation" from Mentoring to Becoming a Colleague

In my own career, I have had many college students move from being my mentees while they were in college or student teaching, to someone much closer to being a colleague, peer, collaborator, and friend. This can only happen over time, and it depends on the relative maturity of the individuals involved. At the college where I teach, many students are non-traditional. Some are my own age or can even be older. This closeness in age, family status, and career stage can help build links that grow into something closer to friendship than mentoring, particularly after the mentees start their own professional careers.

Finding ways to continue to work with mentees as a peer is one of the great rewards for mentors. Watching mentees present at conferences, or co-presenting with them, adds a level of depth to the collaboration. This kind of collaboration also marks a new era of equality in the relationship, since once mentors and mentees start working together, they are having a dialogue of equals about how to do the work, and the mentor needs to admit that he or she can make mistakes as well.

Putting a Period on the Sentence

Likewise, there are some relationships that break down after graduation, and the mentee does not follow the path set out at all. If a mentor provides leads and potential opportunities, only to see the mentee waste or squander them, this can result in a relationship closer to being an acquaintance than a real mentorship. This should not mean permanently cutting someone off, but it can be recognition that the two people involved just disagree on the path to take and are better off with a much less involved relationship than they once had.

Whether for reasons of success or failure of a mentoring relationship, I believe that it pays to put a period on the sentence when it is due. If the relationship is no longer mentor/mentee, marking this transition will help solidify the new relationship. I also believe that people should put the best possible end on the sentence, so that even if the relationship has become tired, or one person has become tired of it, or the mentee does not feel a need for guidance, the two people involved can celebrate their relationship, their time together, and wish one another well. Being able to graciously mark the end of a troubled relationship is an important skill to practice, and while it will feel unpleasant and uncomfortable, it leaves open the door to future, more productive, contact.

Mentees Giving Back: How Will Your Mentee "Pay It Forward" While in College?

The most successful programs we have run have helped mentees become mentors and complete the circle that has benefitted them. In our Young Men's Leadership Program, some of our top high school students started working with middle and elementary school students, delivering the same curriculum they experienced after school. These young men have also been able to return as speakers for our programming, sometimes by Skype, to give other young people the benefit of their experience. At a one-day conference we ran on young men's issues, several of our participants—then in high school—each ran a breakout session, highlighting their talents and offering living proof of our programs' impacts.

Giving young people leadership roles takes them far out of their lives as high school students, and puts them back into the world of middle school students, who often are picked on for no reason by their peers. Learning to respond compassionately when younger boys start to cry while relating stories about being bullied helped the high school students become better young men, and gave the younger students someone to look up to.

Our Upward Bound program now recruits alumni of Upward Bound programs on our campus to come out and mentor high school students. These programs help both groups as the high school students get role models from similar neighborhoods and families, while the college students get to be role models and therefore gain more meaning from their own experiences in being a college student.

Ultimately, any person serving as a mentor in a mentoring program is there because someone invested in him or her. Those we mentor ought to know that. They also should know that, down the line, they should be prepared to give back what they have received from others.

Resource

The Center for the Advancement of Mentoring. *Bringing closure to the mentoring relationship: An overview.* www.nttac.org/media/training Center/149/TCAM%20Bringing%20Closure%20to%20Mentoring%20 Relationships%20Overview%20508%20C.pdf

Building Sustainable Programs

18 How to Know You Are Making a Difference

Mentoring relationships and mentoring programs are difficult to quantify. The impact that one person has on another does not lend itself to the types of analyses that government agencies and other funders like to see. The impact of a positive relationship may not really be seen in full measure for years, although many evaluation projects try to measure the impact of a program only a few months into the effort.

People who want to serve as mentors, and people who start mentoring programs, are not always interested in evaluating or quantifying their impact. This is not to say that they do not want to make an impact, but they are not the same as people who go into medical research, where the relative effectiveness or ineffectiveness of a treatment will make or break one's career.

In spite of the above, mentoring programs and even individual mentors need ways to tell whether what they are doing is having a positive effect, and to make sure they are not having a negative one. This is not to turn your mentoring program into a research study, but to help you better understand how you are doing and to correct for problems that you may see in the program. Furthermore, when it comes to funders, having solid evaluation data is a prerequisite for funding in many areas—from the government, from foundations, even from individuals. Evaluation data allow you to intelligently discuss both your successes and your challenges.

Tools for Evaluation

This chapter will lay out a few tools that individuals and programs can use to track the progress of either a relationship or a program. None of these tools is statistical in nature, and all can be implemented by people who have more of an interest in mentoring than in research design.

The number one rule in evaluation is that the system you set up should be there to help you do a better job. If it is not doing that, think about how to make your system simpler, how to get data more quickly, or how to best turn those data into things you can change about your program.

When to Evaluate

Evaluation systems need to be set up before you start the program. This is never what mentors want to hear, but it is critical to help measure your effectiveness. There is no way to go back in time and get data that you wish you had collected at the start of a program. The data at the start of your program, which evaluators call "baseline data," both helps you to design a program based on participant needs and to measure your progress once you have started.

Key data to collect from participants might include demographics (who is in the program?), data about their current home situations, data about the school setting they attend, information about their health, and even inform-ation about their attitudes. Your emphases will depend on what your program is designed to do. For a program that focuses on college access, you can ask students about their interest in attending college, about what colleges they already know about, and their assessment of whether they will be able to attend.

This information can help you focus resources on topics that really need to be addressed. Early in our GEAR UP program, we realized that the vast majority of our students wanted to go to college. They needed no convincing of the importance of college for their futures. But they did need a lot of work on the academic skills they would need to be successful there. A solid "needs assessment" of the people you are working with can save you from designing a program that no one wants to attend.

In some cases, you may want to collect data or information from parents or teachers of young people as well. Parents are often surprised and flattered to be asked for their opinions about educational topics. Teachers or school administrators are pressed for time, and may require some convincing (or some doughnuts!) to assist in participating. If teachers are able to see that a program is seeking to help their students achieve in school, they are often much more willing to complete a brief survey or assessment.

Evaluating a Single Mentoring Pair

Even as a one-on-one mentor, it pays to keep track of your progress. At the beginning of a relationship, this might include getting some basic information from the student in order to better understand where she or he is academically, socially, at home, and in the community. Once you have decided on a common goal to tackle together, putting this down in writing can serve as a good reference point for future meetings. Then, later develop some next steps for each goal, actions that the mentee can take towards a broader vision. Tracking the achievement of these small objectives over time can lead to larger gains.

 **REAL PEOPLE**

In the Family Empowerment Program that Marquan Jackson runs at Hamilton Crossing in Ypsilanti, Michigan, each family sets goals in the areas of economics, education, and health. Jackson then checks in at least once per quarter on steps being taken towards these goals. Families who have embraced this approach have seen great things happen. Some of his participants have graduated from GED programs, enrolled in college, and several are now off to graduate school. This process helped many people look for and get a job. Documenting the goal and keeping track of the smaller steps gives structure to the process, and then allows the program to look back and document the success of the relationship.

At the close of any mentoring meeting, try to capture any "next steps" you have for a mentee, document these, and come back to them at the next session. It can be a small step, such as turning in an assignment or applications, or setting up a meeting with someone to get more information about a career. But there is something powerful about committing to the goal in writing and to having the mentee be accountable at the next meeting for that step.

Evaluating a Mentoring Program

A mentoring program is really just the sum of its mentoring pairs and groups. If mentoring pairs and groups are setting goals and holding mentees accountable, the overall results are going to be powerful. There are several key ways to capture how a whole program is doing.

Surveys

Surveys are the most cost-effective way of learning about whether a program is being successful or not. Many of our programs use annual surveys to ask participants about their academic achievement, how they feel about school, and how they may be progressing towards their own goals. Surveys, particularly online surveys, are simple to deliver, and such systems as Survey Monkey allow for almost instant analysis of the data, often at low or no cost.

 TIE TO LEADERSHIP

Our office used to spend a good deal of money sending out paper surveys to parents. We no longer do so, since so many were returned due to people moving. We now survey students and teachers at school, and survey parents by phone. We have also had to give people gift cards, food, or other incentives to help make sure we had enough surveys filled out. (We aim for at least a 50 percent response rate.) We try to use surveys that researchers have validated, meaning that it has been shown to test what it is supposed to measure. However, these do not exist for every topic and so in other cases, we have had to write our own.

Surveys give you a very rough idea of whether or not what you are doing in a mentoring program is effective. For instance, ask students their feelings about school at the beginning of a program and again at the end. Or ask them questions that can help you measure how much knowledge they have about a topic you will work on with them (financial aid, for instance). Calculating the difference between the pre-test and the post-test will give you an estimate of the impact you have made on the average participant in the program.

Participation/Satisfaction Data

Many programs, even those run by professionals, fail to capture who participates in the program, and their satisfaction with the program. This makes evaluation of the program impossible. For any program you are running, develop a simple sign-in sheet for mentors and mentees, and make sure these are used at every mentoring activity. The information can then be saved in Excel or a Google spreadsheet for future analysis.

Developing a very simple evaluation (less than a page) for your mentoring events can help as well. If you are hosting a workshop, ask all the young people involved if they found the event valuable, and what they might do to change it for the better. This provides evidence that not only did people attend your programming, but that they got something out of it, at least in the short term.

These participation and satisfaction data help you make the case that your program has caused positive change in the young people you are working with. If you know about the students' knowledge and attitudes before the program, if you know they attended and were engaged with the program, and you know about what they knew and how they felt at the end of the program, you can make a case that your program has had an impact.

Focus Groups

Focus groups are a way of talking to participants in your program to learn more about what they have learned. They are relatively inexpensive to set up (usually food or snacks help get people to attend), and they provide a lot of information and feedback quickly. They are often ideal to help you understand the results of a survey, since you can ask follow-up questions to participants to better understand their answers.

As a rule, it is best to get an outsider to run the focus group, and ask between 5 and 10 participants a series of questions about the program. Unlike a survey, you need to make sure everyone talks at a focus group, and that one or two people do not monopolize the time. Either a recording is made or notes are taken, and these are analyzed for themes and for key ideas. In some cases, these can be rigorously coded using computerized software such as NVivo; in other cases, the notes can be read through quickly to look for major points.

Focus groups are not representative of your whole program. They give the perspectives of the individuals who happened to show up. They can also reflect the direction the conversation took, rather than what people are really thinking. But they are a great tool for understanding what participants find valuable in your program and what they may find problematic. I conducted a focus group for middle school students in one of our after-school programs. I asked them whether they had a day when they only came to school to be part of the after-school program. It turned out that every student had days like that, and a few said it was every day.

More Difficult Analysis: Direct Measures

In many cases, your program may seek to show more than survey data or focus groups. You can also look at direct measures, such as school attendance, grades, ACT scores, admissions to college, and attaining a job. These can be difficult to access and you can have holes in the data as a result. Schools are a particularly difficult source of data, as they are governed by FERPA (Family Education Rights and Privacy Act), which limits the information released from student records.

Students and parents may have some of the data you need, in the form of report cards, progress reports, and online systems. These are not always up to date and accurate, and they can be difficult to get from students and families. However, if you can access these data, you can then begin to make a case for your impact.

A "dosage analysis" looks at how often a student attended or participated in your program, and then looks at the effect on an outcome of interest, such as attendance or school grades. I ran such an analysis for an amazing organization called Mentor 4 Youth that worked with at-risk high school students. If you looked at all their students, the data was mixed. Some participants seemed to bloom while in the program, but others were unaffected. Once we knew which students had participated the most, the data looked much different. Among the students we had worked with the most (four or more months), the students were proven to have fewer absences, fewer tardies to class, and higher grades.

Comparing Participants and Non-Participants

The more difficult and time/labor-intensive forms of evaluation involve comparing people who participate in your program to those who do not. The "gold standard" for evaluation is the randomized controlled study. The population is split into two groups, with one receiving the treatment, the other receiving nothing, each put into a category randomly. People who have a passion for mentoring want to "save them all," and want to accept every young person into a program. They find random assignment heart-wrenching. Some programs have worked around this issue by comparing youth in their programs to youth on a waiting list for the service.

Less rigorous than a control/experimental study is a "matched pair" analysis, which pairs a participant with another person with the same characteristics, such as gender, grades, race, or other status. This is often the best a program can do but relies on having access to a large number of data points to help match the participant and non-participants. The more similar the people in the pairs can be, the more powerful the analysis. With the aid of a research design/statistics specialist, you can also choose other "quasi-experimental" designs, such as comparing students in your program to students on a wait list.

Evaluation Data You Can Use

There are two forms of evaluation data: summative and formative. Summative evaluation occurs at the end of the program or project. It tells you how valuable the program was but only in time for you to do the next project. Formative feedback is the information you get in the middle of the program, which you can use to improve the program, change the program, or even stop it entirely if it is being shown to be ineffective or harmful.

While many programs in the field have strong summative data, I believe that good formative data that is acted upon can really help improve the experience of young people and adults in mentoring programs. Being able to expand on the good, improve the mediocre, and stop poorly performing elements of a program is the sign of a truly excellent program.

Resources

National Center for Women & Information Technology (2011). *Evaluating a mentoring program.* www.ncwit.org/sites/default/files/resources/evaluating mentoringprogramguide_web.pdf

National Mentoring Partnership. *Start a program: Evaluation.* www.mentoring. org/start_a_program/evaluation

19 | Get the Word Out!
Marketing Mentoring Programs

People genuinely interested in mentoring are not always the best marketers of their efforts. Many would even find the idea of marketing repulsive, since they are focused on improving the lives of young people, not in making a bigger name for themselves or for the organization. Many who believe in servant leadership stick with the idea that the best leader makes him or herself an almost invisible support to those he or she is assisting. In many religious and spiritual traditions, anonymous assistance is preferable to making a big deal out of one's generosity.

While all the above positions are valid, and are often deeply felt, they can greatly limit what an organization can do, particularly when it comes to seeking support and resources. I often have to tell people I work with that while I admire and value their personal modesty, it is not helping them develop their program. Taken to an extreme, efforts become invisible.

Good marketing for a mentoring program starts with being clear and being honest about what you are seeking to accomplish and what impact you are having. This can even include challenges that you have not yet surmounted, if you want to be as balanced as possible.

Tell People What You Are Doing

There are many different constituencies for even a small mentoring program. Participants need to know what is going on in the program, including when and where to show up. Parents might need information about what the program is doing and how they can help. There are always community leaders and elected officials, even at the school and local level, who would love to be kept in the loop about what you are doing, if only so that they can answer other people's questions about the program if asked.

If you do not run a large organization, pieces of communication can work for more than one audience. Many groups use a regular newsletter to update everyone on upcoming events, then forward this to their program officer and others at their institution. Social media have opened up many more platforms for organizations to use and reuse material. For example, a photo from an event can be sent out immediately on Instagram, then form part of a Facebook update later, end up in an email newsletter, and finally reside on a webpage.

For younger audiences, marketing should be more immediate and more casual. For those in their teens and 20s, raised in a world of electronic media, a paper newsletter is something from a time capsule. They want to see what is going on at the program in real time. They also want to hear about things "word of mouth," or one participant emailing, Tweeting, or Instagramming about the event while it is happening, not an official email a few days later from program staff.

Crafting a Message

Every mentoring organization needs to be able to explain what it does, how it does it, why it does so, and what effect it has. This does not mean investing in a massive strategic plan or devising a whole media campaign. But when you are at a meeting, you should be able to explain a lot about your organization in a few short sentences. The sentences you say should not be completely different from what the other people in your organization say and your participants report. Devising this quick "elevator speech" is a good investment of time and energy, as a two-hour meeting can produce a very useful piece of text for the whole organization.

This process can help you focus on exactly what your organization is trying to do. Reduce crime? Keep participants safe after school? Build academic achievement? All of the above? Getting your message down to a few sentences will help everyone see better what you do and what you are not trying to accomplish.

This can change in emphasis over time. In the Bright Futures after-school program at EMU, they have focused on adding elements, based on the latest research, to the program to help young people succeed. This objective statement has been added to their list of what they do: "To develop grit and a growth mindset through trying new things, perseverance, and the belief that ability and skill are developed through dedication to hard work."

This level of specificity helps people understand the program focus and to connect them to like-minded individuals and groups.

 REAL PEOPLE

Tips from a Professional in the Field

Linette Lao's company, Invisible Engines, helps non-profits market themselves. She told me that many community programs have trouble telling their story in clear and interesting ways, resorting to "institutional" language that talks down to people. Lao told me: "There are more ways than ever for organizations to get stories out."

Particularly for younger people, a good web and social-media presence are requirements. While many organizations are trapped in a world of brochures and newsletters, participants in mentoring programs and supporters of them have moved out into the digital world, where immediate information is more important. "You are doing a disservice to your program by not pushing out the stories in your program," she says, which can include blogs, guest blogs, social media, web pages, or email marketing.

Lao's marketing tips for organizations include:

- Sometimes an outsider, while an extra expense, can put her or his finger on what is really remarkable about a program in a way that the staff or participants cannot.
- High-quality photographs taken by a professional photographer who has an eye for human interaction can make all the difference. It is not just a matter of the camera, but the aesthetic that the person brings to it.
- Marketing should be scalable and cost effective. Many digital tools, such as Facebook or Twitter, are relatively inexpensive to develop. Blogs, in which participants can be "guest bloggers," can also be effective.

Examples of Good Marketing and Recruiting

Big Brothers/Big Sisters, one of the oldest mentoring organizations in existence, has spent a lot of time and effort honing its message. As it seeks to pair each child with an adult "big," the recruiting needs of the organization are massive. Right now they are looking for 30,000 Bigs to pair with Littles. On their website, their tagline "Start something for a child today" both says something about what the group does (help children) and stresses the immediacy of the effort (start something today).

On a smaller scale, Champions of Wayne is a privately funded mentoring program in Wayne, Michigan, which pairs students with a mentor to take on a challenge. It also provides a small financial reward if the challenge is met. Director Sean Galvin, lacking a large budget, developed a Facebook page and Twitter feed for the group, providing quick updates and opportunities to participate in and support the program. The site also provides tips, information, and congratulations as mentees meet their goals.

Melissa Calabrese's Bright Futures site provides almost daily photos of what students are up to. As a result, sometimes I know more about her students' activities than about my daughter's day at school.

Try Anything

A partial list of some of the things we have tried in terms of marketing our programs:

- Asking a local coffee shop to hang photos of our program activities or taken by program youth.
- Marching in the local July 4 parade.
- Spots on a local radio station to promote parenting strategies.
- Posting messages on our university's electronic bulletin boards.
- Facebook, Twitter, and Instagram feeds of program information.
- Videos of our NASA STEM project posted on YouTube.
- Videos of our students' speeches on the TedEd and YouTube networks.

Things to Avoid in Marketing Your Program

Every mentoring program needs a photo/video release form for students and their families to fill out, and a system to make sure that no one who has opted out of having his or her image used is put into publicity for the program.

While it can be tricky, try to make your marketing materials as positive as possible, without undue negativity towards other organizations. While your local school system may have less than stellar graduation rates, calling them "failures" in a presentation will not do you any good.

Not everything in your program needs to be perfect. Statements that 100 percent of your students graduate from high school and move on to the Ivy Leagues will raise more suspicions than dollars. Balance your message: give both your achievements and your very real challenges.

Resources

National Collaborative on Workforce and Disability. *Marketing your mentoring program.* www.ncwd-youth.info/assets/guides/mentoring/Mentoring-Chapter_7.pdf

Virginia Mentoring Partnership. *Marketing concepts for mentoring programs.* www.ncwd-youth.info/assets/guides/mentoring/Mentoring-Chapter_7.pdf

National Collaborative on Workforce and Disability. "Chapter 10: Marketing a HS/HT program" in Rhodes, S. (2007). *High school/high tech program guide.* www.dol.gov/odep/documents/a6906418_b620_4d70_bcba_52dd c3ef35a9.pdf

20 | Finding Resources for Mentoring Programs

In a perfect world, mentoring would be an area that was well funded. Since mentoring has a positive track record in improving academic success, helping in social adjustment, and preventing crime, you would think that government and other funders would be actively seeking investment opportunities in the field. Given that alternatives to mentoring include dropping out of high school (this costs society over $1 million over a lifetime) or incarceration (which costs $31,286 per inmate per day), if mentoring programs could access even a fraction of what they saved governments, they would be flush with cash.

In most cases, mentoring programs are relatively difficult to fund, and government agencies have funded them at level amounts or cut them over the past decades. This means that mentoring programs need to be savvy about where they seek the resources they need. Below is a short guide to where mentoring efforts might find funding, whether large or small in size and scope.

Type of Funding

Many mentoring programs look to outside funding to either start or expand operations. The most logical place to look for funding is grants, either from a unit of government (federal, state, or local), from foundations or other community funders, or from individuals. The most basic distinction is that a grant is a payment from one organization to another that is really a payment for something done. It is a contract that lays out what work will occur and how it will be paid for. This is different from a gift, which does not have the same contractual agreement, although a gift can be restricted in terms of what it can be spent on.

Straightforward Funding: Asking for Help

Particularly for small organizations, grants can be more of a headache than they are worth for mentoring programs. Many funders require that an organization receive its 501c3 (indicating official non-profit status) before applying for a grant, and some require an annual audit. For a small organization, such as one that has only a paid executive director, these requirements can make grants a losing proposition, as the organization can incur thousands of dollars of spending in order to become eligible to apply for a grant that they may not receive.

For smaller organizations, asking directly for help from service clubs, individuals, or community groups may make more sense at the start of an effort. Mentoring programs are labor intensive, but not expensive in terms of materials and supplies. Often what might be needed to get underway might be incentives for participants, program supplies, transportation, and free low-cost activities. While service clubs such as Rotary are often overlooked by smaller organizations, they can provide a good platform for recognition, as well as a source of small amounts of funding. Community groups such as the United Way may be able to provide seed funding in key strategic areas.

Individual donors and clubs can also make a big difference. There are many individuals who have had positive experiences being mentored who may be willing to make an investment in your community. Seeking these people out, getting their ideas, and asking for support can be critical. There are many businesses that really embrace having a double-bottom line—doing good while they are making a profit—and these can be tapped for help. Some companies are generous in allowing employees to donate time while on the job, and some companies fund efforts that employees support, either in grants or matching employee gifts. In some communities, "giving circles" have taken root, allowing organizations to pitch their idea one evening over dinner, and potentially walk away with a few thousand dollars in funding.

While it is psychologically difficult to ask people face to face for financial support, the money you raise in this way can help your program, and those individuals and groups can help you seek further funding. Even traditional fundraising, such as bowling, car washes, and 5k runs can help raise some needed funds, as well as provide visibility for your program in the community.

Grants

Writing a grant can be the most straightforward way to seek external funding for a mentoring program. Government agencies usually offer Requests for Proposals (RFPs) that seek programs that accomplish certain activities, and there is a dollar amount attached to these. For a complex federal grant, the application may run over 100 pages, while for a less complicated effort, five pages of narrative may be all that is required.

Many grants, whether they say so or not, require some form of pilot data to show that you know that your methodology will work. Some require a needs assessment to show that you know what you are up against. All funders require that you show that there is a need for your project, some sort of gap between the way things are and the way that things could be if they implemented your program. Grant applications require a solid work plan, a thorough budget, and a description of the organization and people who will do the work on the project.

For smaller organizations, grants can be a punishing form of seeking funds. The requirements for spending grant dollars might include accounting that a smaller organization is not prepared to take on. Writing a grant can be a major effort, and some organizations hire a grant writer to try to win funding. For a first grant, it may make sense to find a partner organization willing to help with the parts you are weak in, and provide a recognizable name for the funder.

Social Enterprise

Some funders, tired of putting agencies onto a treadmill of continually seeking grants for funding, have tried to develop new methods of funding important social programs. Social enterprise is a way of trying to find ways for programs to be more sustainable from the beginning, sometimes by taking on more businesslike aspects. Mentoring programs may use job training as a way of creating products, which then can be sold to help fund the organization.

In some cases, funders seek to create systems where successful programs are paid based on their evaluation metrics (pay for success), which is connected to the cost savings for the project. For example, better social-service programs in low-income housing could cut down on emergency room visits, saving money for the health-care system. The documented reduction in these visits would lead to more funding for social agencies that produced this result.

Social-impact bonds are another way of capturing savings. Investors would make funding for programs upfront, and if they were successful, would receive payments from the government based on the cost savings. For instance, a mentoring program that cut recidivism for youth involved in the juvenile justice system would receive funding based on what it would have cost to incarcerate the youth. In a social-impact bond arrangement, investors who put their money behind these efforts would be paid back their investment, plus interest, based on these results.

Social enterprise is an emerging field, and there is a lot of excitement behind it. It offers ways of running programs that can be financially supported over the long haul, sometimes with the use of a business that supports the non-profit activities. However, some people and funders just do not know what to do with a social enterprise, so the path, for now, is less explored than the traditional non-profit option.

Foundations

Unlike grants, foundation money is based on relationships and on the priorities of the grantor at the moment. Foundations can range from tiny family foundations, which may not have a single employee, to vast organizations that control billions of dollars. In all cases, it pays to build a solid relationship with a foundation before asking for funds, and then to continue to cultivate that relationship as you seek and are granted money.

While foundations can give large or multi-year grants, they often seek to fund programs at modest levels at first, and to look to make investments in an agency for a short period of time. For mentoring programs, foundation funding might be a great opportunity to expand programming or to seek ways to improve what the program does. It is less often a source of the long-term operational funds that programs may need year after year.

TIE TO LEADERSHIP

Simple Tools to Develop

If you are seeking funding for a program, the following tools will help you no matter the avenue from which you seek your dollars:

1. A one-page document that lays out what your program seeks to do, how it accomplishes this, and basic numbers about the program (e.g.,

number of young people served), as well as some quotes from participants (if you have them and have their permission). These one-page documents can be used with donors, as discussion starters with funders.

2. A quick sentence or two, on the tip of your tongue, about what your program seeks to do. This elevator pitch is often needed on the spur of the moment to clarify what your program really does and why it is important to fund. You should never underestimate how easy it is for a donor or potential supporter to pass you by just because she or he cannot really understand what you are trying to accomplish.

3. As soon as you can get it, have some simple evaluation metrics you can share with people, such as:
   - 20 students attended our summer camp
   - 4 students saw their GPA rise by over one whole grade point
   - 60 percent of our students reported that they felt better about school.

There is no need to be fancy, and the data need not be all good news, but having some key numbers at your fingerprints shows people that you are serious about what you are doing.

Resources

National Mentoring Partnership. *Finding resources to support mentoring programs and services for youth.* www.mentoring.org/downloads/mentoring_1154.pdf

Office of Juvenile Justice and Delinquency Prevention. *Mentoring resources.* www.ojjdp.gov/programs/mentoring.html

Philanthropy News Digest. *RFPs.* http://philanthropynewsdigest.org/rfps